THE JOURNEY TO WEALTH

The Journey *to* Wealth

Smart Investment Strategies to Stay Ahead of the Curve

JAMES E. DEMMERT

NEW INSIGHTS
PRESS

Editorial Direction and Editing: Rick Benzel
Art Direction and Design: Susan Shankin & Associates
Illustrations & Graphics: Tim Kummerow

Published by New Insights Press
Los Angeles, CA

Second Printing
Printed at Bang Printing in the United States of America
Library of Congress Control Number: 2016945185
ISBN 978-0-9973357-1-2

Seven Deadly Sins

Wealth without Work

Pleasure without Conscience

Science without Humanity

Knowledge without Character

Politics without Principle

Commerce without Morality

Worship without Sacrifice

—MAHATMA GANDHI

Preface

ARE YOU INTERESTED IN LEARNING
the key concepts that make for successful
investing and wealth management? If so,
I invite you to read and enjoy this book. It
reflects my three plus decades of investment
knowledge and wealth management experience.
My goal is to help people grow their wealth
by seeking out the most successful long-term,
goal-oriented investment performance, amidst
a high level of risk management.

My process of managing wealth is in many
ways unique. In this book, I share the intricacies
of the process I have created and why I believe
that success as an investor in today's financial
markets requires going against much of Wall
Street's so-called "wisdom."

I will show you why most investors tend to
have below average results, and how my philosophy and strategies can improve your investment
process and performance. Many investors tend
to repeat the same mistakes, yet these can be
avoided. Wall Street is full of popular investment
theories that just do not work. I dispel for you
many of these theories and provide details about
a process that can help you become a better
investor, whether you do it yourself or use a
financial professional.

We will examine the fundamental concepts of "risk" and "return," which are central
to making wise investment decisions. You will
learn how to benefit from knowing exactly how
financial markets work and how to use this

knowledge to your advantage. There are many types of investment instruments, and each has pros and cons you should know about. I will discuss why the "average" investor overpays for their investments and how that leads directly to poor results. Most Wall Street firms have embraced investment products such as mutual funds and exchange traded funds as an easy way to "set it and forget it" when they create client portfolios. You will see the flaws of this approach as I introduce you to a different way of thinking and a process that provides a greater possibility of return, more transparency and stronger risk management.

It is obvious that today's investment markets are very risky compared to previous decades. However, I continue to meet investors who take on more risk than they need while having a gross lack of risk management. I believe in clearly defining your risk parameters and understanding the tools that you can use to mitigate catastrophic loss. Risk management, in any form, appears to be what today's investors lack most—but it is what is most needed!

We will also take an in-depth look at "investor psychology"—the subjective and emotional motivators that drive many investors to make bad decisions in periods of euphoria and good times, as well as during periods of panic and crisis. There are lessons you can learn about your own psychology and how not to fall for the little voice in your head telling you what to do out of fear or greed.

Understanding the history of the financial markets is a foundational key to investing. This is one of the most important elements of my philosophy. Through the study of history, you can discover meaningful patterns—regular ups and downs in the market that happen at what appear to be predictable times. They are so pronounced that they are often called market cycles. Many people are not aware of these cycles, and since investors are not students of history, they are doomed to repeat mistakes. Too many investors make the same mistakes by failing to recognize these cycles or take advantage of them.

Throughout this book, I will illustrate the importance of creating your own "wealth plan"— a well thought-out and proactive strategy to guide your investment process. This book will help you develop a better understanding of how to invest, when to invest, where to invest and in what types of securities. Along with many insights into the process that I use to select securities and alternative investments, you will learn how to maximize your returns while managing your own downside risk to avoid catastrophic loss.

I strongly believe it is better to have a prosperous society than a struggling one. People at all income levels need to understand investing so they can build the assets they need to provide for their families, educate their children, and ensure that they have enough income saved for retirement and financial independence.

Many people are daunted by investing, and scared of learning more about it, feeling they cannot master it. To transform investing into an enjoyable topic, each chapter in this book aims to help you overcome any trepidation you may have. I have sought to make it fun to read, with many sidebars, quotes and some humor, special features, illustrations and graphical presentations, and more.

I invite you to keep this book on your coffee table, at your bedside, or on your desk at work, and browse through it from time to time to enjoy the great quotes about investing, the artwork, and the wisdom you will learn about the right way to grow wealth.

Here's to your financial future!

JAMES E. DEMMERT

37.8591° N

122.4853° W

For centuries, most investors—individual and institutional—have fallen victim to buying high and selling low. Why? Human psychology is not geared to prudent investing. Most investors have short-term memories and/or have not been investors long enough to know the market's history. It is common for most investors to be unaware of how much return and corresponding risk they require, which leads them into trouble. Add to this a general lack of "investment process" and no use of risk management tools, and you get poor results, if not catastrophic loss. These have devastating long-term implications.

As part of my philosophy, I use history, psychology, research and risk management tools to help investors take the journey to wealth.

CHAPTER ONE

Fundamentals *of* Investing

MARKETS, RISKS AND REWARDS

> "The biggest risk is not taking risk.... in a world that is changing really quickly, the only strategy that is guaranteed to fail is not taking a risk.
>
> —*Mark Zuckerberg, CEO Facebook*"

Investing

What it means, what it does

Wealth...the dream that most people have to be able to live without concern about how to pay for their needs and their luxuries. What people consider wealth varies. For some, having $500,000 satisfies their sense of being wealthy, while for others, $5,000,000 only begins to approach the borderline of wealth.

No matter how much wealth you desire, you need to understand and practice **investing.** Unless you plan to collect your wealth in dollar bills and store them under your mattress, or put them in a metal box and bury them in a hole in the ground, you need to do something to grow your money. And whatever you do with it is called investing.

Money isn't everything, but happiness alone can't keep out the rain.

This is not a book to prescribe how much wealth you should have. That is your decision. Franklin D. Roosevelt reminded us that, "Happiness is not in the mere possession of money; it lies in the joy of achievement, in the thrill of creative effort."

The dictionary defines investing as, *"To put money to use, by purchase or expenditure, in something offering potential profitable returns, as interest, income, or appreciation in value."* In short, investing takes the money you have today and attempts to make it become worth more.

In this sense, we can say that investing does three simple things for you:

- **It acts as a time machine.** Investing helps savers transport their surplus income from today into the future. It gives today's borrowers access to future earnings now.

- **It acts as a safety net.** Investing insures people against the loss of income from illness, job loss, unplanned events, and even from the costs of floods, fires or other disasters.

- **It acts as an engine of growth.** Investors can seek out those people and companies with innovative new ideas, and use their capital to finance those ideas to create new products and services that can create more wealth.

By providing these three kinds of functions, a well-tuned investing system smooths out your life's sharpest ups and downs, making an uncertain world more predictable.

How Money Grows

Two essential ways to make money work for you

Invested money works for you. It may grow a little or a lot, depending on where you invest it. But the most fundamental idea to understand now is that any money you can invest today will be worth more tomorrow . . . and even more next year . . . and ten years from now, whoa, it can be worth much more. By investing your money, you are getting it to generate more by earning interest on what you put away or through your buying and selling assets that increase in value over time.

In contrast, if you keep your funds in your back pocket instead of investing them, they won't work for you and you will never have more money than what you put into your pocket.

Whether your goal is to send your kids to college or to retire on a yacht in the Mediterranean, investing is essential to getting you to where you want to be.

There are two ways your assets can work for you when you invest:

- **Your money earns money.** Someone pays you to use your funds for a period of time. You then get your money back plus "interest." Or, if you buy stock in a company that pays "dividends" to shareholders, the company pays you a portion of its earnings on a regular basis. Now your funds are making an "income."

- **You buy something with your money that "appreciates," i.e., it increases in value.** You become an owner of something that you can sell for a greater value later. All the following items have the potential to appreciate: stocks, mutual funds, coins, artwork, wine, real estate, collectibles, gemstones, antiques and rare items, and more.

PRINCIPLE 1
HAVING MONEY MEANS YOU MAY NOT NEED TO WORK

One of the most compelling reasons for you to invest is the prospect of not having to work your entire life! Bottom line, there are only two ways to make money: by working and/or by having your assets work for you. If you can make your money work for you—and generate enough income per year, you can stop working and do the things in life you most want to do.

Should You Take More or Less Risk?

Neither . . . take SMART risks

Some types of investments have very little risk. For example, if you invest in a bank savings account that is secure and guaranteed to pay you interest every month, there is little risk and thus only a small reward. If you invest in bonds that a company or a government entity issues, there is slightly more risk than a savings account, so the rewards are slightly better. If you invest in stocks, real estate, wine, artwork, or other financial instruments, there is a lot more risk, since the growth in value (appreciation) of these investments is uncertain and cannot be predicted. Your investment could grow in value—or it could tank! As a result, higher risk investments tend to yield greater rewards as a way to entice investors to take those risks.

My goal here is to teach people how to grow their investments to achieve the highest rewards by taking **SMART** risks, based on psychology, market cycles and extensive research. Throughout the rest of this book, I will describe my philosophy to build your wealth.

What I Mean By "SMART" Investing

S **Strategic.** You have enough knowledge to make good strategic decisions about how and where you invest your money

M **Modeling.** You are able to make good predictions based on financial models of how your money will grow for you.

A **Attention.** You or someone you hire will track your investments and make adjustments as needed to take advantage of the market and minimize your risks.

R **Reliability.** You are working with a philosophy of investing that is reliable; you can count on it to work, whether we are in a bull or bear market.

T **Trust.** You trust yourself or those involved in your investment decisions so that you have complete peace of mind that your money is safe and secure.

Fortune sides with him who dares.
—VIRGIL

A Savings Account: The Simplest Way of Investing

The difference between simple vs. compound interest

Let's start with the safest way to grow your money—a bank savings account or a Certificate of Deposit (CD). You're probably familiar with a savings account. A CD is like a special savings account in which you invest a fixed amount that might range from $1,000 to $50,000, and it must remain in that account for a fixed period of time, which might range from 6 months to 5 years. Some CDs let you liquidate your money in advance if you pay a small penalty.

When you invest in these types of instruments, the best way to speed up the growth of your money is to ensure that you are earning "compound interest," not "simple interest."

Simple interest means that the principal of your investment earns whatever percentage the account agrees to pay. If you invest $10,000 (your principal), and the bank pays 3% per year simple interest, you will earn $300 for each year you keep the money in that account.

Compound interest is a step higher in **SMART** investing. With compound interest, you earn interest on the money you put into the account, *plus* on the interest that the money has earned. For example, $10,000 in principal that earns 3% per year becomes $10,300 after one year. But in the second year, you will earn 3% interest on the $10,300, not just on the original $10,000. In other words, with compound interest, your principal grows each year as the prior year's interest gets added to it. Each year, you are therefore earning interest on all the interest you already earned.

Over time, even a small percentage of compounded interest continuously earned can add up to big money and help you achieve your financial goals. For example, compare the two scenarios in the table below about investing $10,000 at simple vs. compound interest for 30 years.

As you can see, at the end of 30 years, an account paying 3% simple interest yields $19,000 while an account paying 3% compound interest yields $24,273, a difference of $5,273.

	Simple Interest				Compound Interest		
Time	Principal at start of that year	Interest earned @ 3% per year	Total savings at end of that year		Principal amount at start of that year	Interest earned @ 3% per year compounded	Total savings at end of that year
1	$10,000	$300	$10,300		$10,000	$300	$10,300
2	$10,000	$300	$10,600		$10,300	$309	$10,609
3	$10,000	$300	$10,900		$10,609	$318	$10,927
10	$10,000	$300	$13,000		$13,048	$391	$13,439
20	$10,000	$300	$16,000		$17,535	$526	$18,061
30	$10,000	$300	$19,000		$23,566	$709	$24,273
		TOTAL SAVINGS	$19,000			TOTAL SAVINGS	$24,273

Compound interest rather than simple interest can make a big difference in your savings over time. Here $10,000 earning 3% per year becomes $24,273 with compound interest versus $19,000 with simple interest after 30 years.

Look at the compound interest curve below. Its line shoots up at a much steeper climb than the line for simple interest. This is called the "compound interest curve," and is worth remembering when you decide to save money in an interest-bearing account. Be sure that you are receiving compound interest any time you invest in a savings account or Certificate of Deposit.

Monthly compounding

There are bank savings accounts and other investment instruments that pay you interest every month, and they compound that interest on a monthly basis. As you might imagine, monthly compounding is even better than yearly compounding, because every single month, you are earning interest on top of the prior month's interest. As the chart on the prior page shows, $10,000 invested in a savings account that pays 3% interest compounded yearly returns $24,272.62 in 30 years. But if this savings account paid you 3% interest and compounded it monthly, you'd end up with $24,568.42 instead—an extra $295.80 for you.

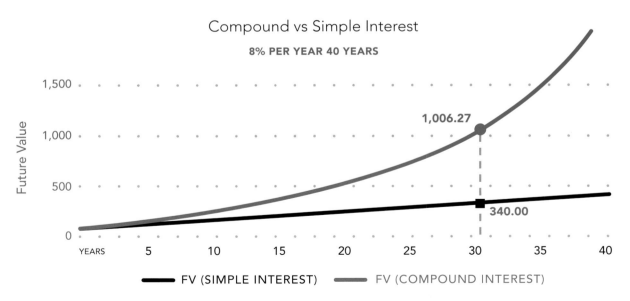

Compound vs Simple Interest
8% PER YEAR 40 YEARS

The compound interest curve rises sharply over simple interest as a savings account starting with $100 earns interest on the interest each year. Here, this chart compares simple vs. compound interest paid at 8% per year.

The Rule of 72

Mathematical magic to predict how fast you can double your money

One of the best ways to estimate how much money you can end up with when you are earning compound interest is the rule of 72. This rule is like mathematical magic in that it helps you quickly estimate how many years it will take you to double your investment, given a specific interest rate. The rule is based on a formula: divide the interest rate into 72 and the result is the approximate number of years it will take you to double your money. (The result is slightly off from the actual mathematical answer, but is a good ballpark estimate.)

For example, if you have $10,000 and want to know about how long it will take to double that amount at a 2% compound interest rate, divide 72 by 2 and you get 36 years. That's a long time!

But if you take the same $10,000 and instead earned an 8% interest rate, it would take you only about 9 years to double your money (72/8 = 9). Who wouldn't prefer 9 years over 36 years?

The more time you have available to grow your money, the less money you need to start with, because compounding interest will be hard at work for you the entire time. For instance, if you want $500,000 in 10 years, you would need to invest $250,000 today and get a 7.2% interest rate. But if you have 20 years to grow that same $500,000, you would only need to start with a $125,000 investment at that same 7.2% interest rate.

Again, the rule of 72 is an approximation, but it helps you quickly estimate three types of calculations:

- You can calculate the number of years it will take to double your money at any given interest rate.

- Or you can calculate what interest rate you need to double your money at any given number of years.

- Or you can calculate how much money you need today to achieve a certain goal in the future at a given interest rate.

The Rule of SMART Investing vs. The Rule of 72

The BIG question: How fast do you want to make money?

The rule of 72 teaches us that when interest rates on savings accounts are low, it takes a very long time to double your money. If you are 30 years old and you earn only 2% on a savings account, whatever the amount, you will be 66 years old by the time your money is doubled.

But the rule of 72 also helps you understand that if you can earn 8%, 10%, 12% . . . or more, you can double your money in less than 10 years.

PRINCIPLE 2
THE FUNDAMENTAL CHOICE IN INVESTING: RISK VS. REWARD

The driving force in investing is to grow your investment. There's no debate about this. But how fast you grow it is the perennial dilemma for all investors. There is a fundamental choice every investor must make: risk versus reward. In general, the more risk you take, the greater the reward. The less risk you take, the less the reward.

But the question is:

Where can you get a return of 8%, 10%, or more?

That's where SMART investing comes in.

Where SMART Investors Go to Find Higher Rates of Return

Lots of choices, lots of confusion

There are many types of investments, such as stocks, bonds, real estate, treasury bills, etc., that yield higher rates of return than savings accounts or CDs. I will explain the different types of market investments in the coming chapters, but for now, here's a brief look at each.

- **Individual common stocks.** Since the 1920s, there have been many periods of time when the stock market as a whole advanced by more than 10% annually. Every year, there are thousands of companies whose stocks grow by 10%, 20%, or even as high as 100% in a single year. People who invest wisely by choosing the right individual common stocks, and hold those stocks for the right amount of time, can easily achieve an average return greater than 8% across an entire portfolio of stocks. However, with these returns comes risk—there are periods when individual stocks or the whole stock market declines dramatically.

- **Treasury, Corporate and Municipal Bonds.** Corporations and federal, state and municipal governments often need to borrow money for their investments and operations. To do so, they may issue a "bond," which is a promise to pay an investor back the amount due at a future date, plus interest paid quarterly or semi-annually during the holding period. For example, you may purchase a two-year bond today for $10,000 and you will receive 3% interest each year you own the bond. At bond maturity, you then get your $10,000 back. These loans to the federal government, corporations and municipalities range in duration from one month up to 30 years. These bonds can have a face (par) value of $1,000 up to $5,000,000.

- **Index funds.** These are funds composed of many different stocks selected to imitate the movement of the entire stock market, or a balance between stocks and bonds.

For example, when you invest in an S&P 500 Index fund, you are buying a fund that seeks to perform exactly like the 500 largest stocks in the US. Historically speaking (between 1926 and 2010), the S&P 500 Index has had an average annualized return of 9.87%, so choosing one of these index funds is one way to obtain a greater than 8% return. Index funds have fees called expense ratios.

- **Mutual funds.** These are funds composed of many different stocks and/or bonds that a financial advisor or a financial company has selected. There are literally thousands of mutual funds to choose from, and each has its own investment profile and historical track record. Each mutual fund has a manager whose responsibility is to grow the fund according to its charter. Some mutual funds are aimed at "growth," meaning the manager's goal is to choose stocks that will appreciate in value over time. Other mutual funds are "income" funds, meaning the manager's goal is to choose securities that pay dividends and thus produce income for you. Still other mutual funds are a blend of these and are called "growth and income" funds, because the manager's goal is to produce both growth and dividends. The value of a mutual fund is established only once per day, at the end of the day, based on the cumulative value of the securities and investments within. Mutual funds, like index funds, have fees associated with their management called expense ratios or management fees. These fees range from .50% to as high as 2% annually.

- **Exchange traded funds (ETFs).** These are a hybrid type of investment that combines features of both stocks and mutual funds. ETFs are like mutual funds in that they can be composed of one or more types of securities (stocks, bonds, currency, gold, oil futures) all in one basket. But more like stocks, an ETF is traded throughout the day, so its price fluctuates with market demand, compared to mutual funds which are valued only at the end of the day. Like index and mutual funds, there are fees associated with exchange traded funds.

Comparing Historical Returns of Different Asset Classes

The big surprise: stocks perform the best

Given that investors have a choice of many financial instruments for their portfolio, it is useful to compare all the asset classes potentially available from a birds-eye view. Which perform the best over time? The chart on the next page provides excellent insight into the answer. It compares the average annual return of many leading asset classes over 41 years between 1975 and 2016. As you can see, the bars on the chart show the average return of each asset class as well as the "real" return after inflation.

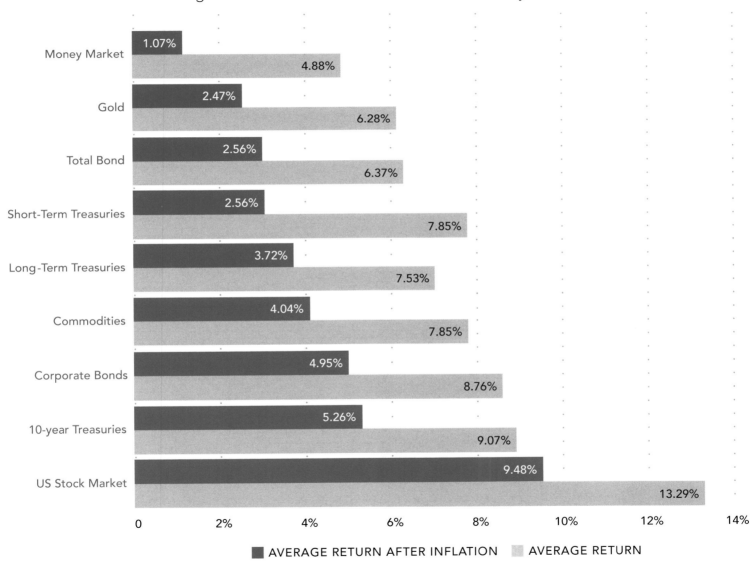

Average Annual Historical Returns 1975–2016 of Major Investment Asset Classes

Asset Class	Average Return After Inflation	Average Return
Money Market	1.07%	4.88%
Gold	2.47%	6.28%
Total Bond	2.56%	6.37%
Short-Term Treasuries	2.56%	7.85%
Long-Term Treasuries	3.72%	7.53%
Commodities	4.04%	7.85%
Corporate Bonds	4.95%	8.76%
10-year Treasuries	5.26%	9.07%
US Stock Market	9.48%	13.29%

■ AVERAGE RETURN AFTER INFLATION   ■ AVERAGE RETURN

Using Stocks as the Primary Investment for Growth in a Portfolio

I carefully research and select stocks

As you can see from the chart on the previous page, the stock market is, by far, the most advantageous instrument to have as the key component in your investment portfolio. A quick glance at the chart proves that stocks have performed better than any other asset class over the long run. Consider these comparisons:

- Stocks have far and away outperformed bonds, which have much less volatility, but have produced results far short of stocks.

- Gold has skyrocketed from time to time, but it has also experienced many years of losses and so it pales in comparison to stocks.

- Money market funds have produced the lowest returns, though they have the least amount of volatility and risk.

The moral of the story is that **SMART** investors must seek the highest possible returns while minimizing risks. A savings account or CD may offer security because it guarantees the payment of interest, but these investments usually pay a very low rate. They may be a good choice if you have 40 or 50 years to save and don't want to take any risks. However, most of us do not have this much time, as we are investing across a 5– to 30–year time frame.

On the other hand, investing in the stock market through the use of individual stocks can yield the highest annual rates of return, ranging from 8% to 15%. But the stock market carries more risks of volatility and potential market declines of up to 50% that can take years to recover from, yielding no return. These down periods completely negate the rule of 72, which is predicated on consistent annual returns. The rule of 72 works to your advantage only if you are participating in an advancing market that has no treacherous or lengthy declines. The often touted rule of 72 can be manipulated to sound great by unscrupulous financial advisors who aim to persuade you that historical stock market returns can go on forever. But they fail to inform investors that there are often long periods when stock markets decline and take years to recover.

This is why I believe that a prudent and carefully selected combination of high-quality stocks, combined with more conservative investments, is the key to long-term wealth building. Seldom does a portfolio 100% invested in CDs/ bonds, or a portfolio of 100% stocks, lead to long-term success. Ideally, when a combination of asset classes is strategically adjusted based on market conditions, the long-term results will be even greater.

The **SMART** use of stocks and the combination of asset classes is the core of my investment philosophy. The key is to select high quality stocks as the centerpiece of your portfolio, and monitor and adjust those stock choices based on extensive research and attention to market conditions to minimize the risks of loss, while maintaining a calculated portion of each portfolio in conservative asset classes. At all times, the goal is to seek the highest annualized returns at the lowest risk by mitigating years of negative or zero return. Only then can the magic of the rule of 72 play a role in helping build real wealth.

> **SUCCESS PRODUCES SUCCESS, JUST AS MONEY PRODUCES MONEY.**
> —DIANE ACKERMAN

A Brief History of Stock Market Exchanges

Stock markets originated to provide investors with an opportunity to share in the profits of public enterprises. Companies needed capital, and offered "shares" of their ownership to the public, who could buy and trade the shares through a central clearinghouse—the stock market. The Amsterdam Stock Exchange (1602) is considered to be the first to allow investors to buy and sell shares in a commercial enterprise—in this case, the Dutch East India Company, which sent trading ships to the East Indies and Asia. Investors purchased shares in future voyages, and received dividends from the proceeds of successful ones (or ate the losses from unsuccessful ones)! The stock shares could also be bought and sold among investors, just like stock markets today.

London became the second major stock exchange to be set up in Europe (1773). In the US, it was Philadelphia that opened the first public stock market exchange (1790) followed shortly thereafter by the New York Stock Exchange (1792), which established itself on Wall Street because it was a central location for all business and trade coming into and leaving colonial America.

Over the next two centuries, the NYSE grew to become the world's leading stock exchange. Many other countries founded exchanges, too, including France, Germany, Switzerland, Canada, South Africa, Hong Kong, Japan, Australia and China, but the NYSE has largely dominated all other exchanges in terms of where the largest companies of the world seek to list their stocks for trade.

In 1971, a new exchange emerged, founded by the National Association of Securities Dealers, and became known as The NASDAQ. This exchange had no physical residence or trading floor, only a network of computers on which securities dealers could electronically execute trades of stock shares. The NASDAQ

was originally the preferred market for smaller companies to list their shares. Now it is best known as the exchange where new high technology companies launch their Initial Public Offering (IPO), including Apple, Facebook, eBay, PayPal and many others.

When you invest in individual stocks, it doesn't matter which stock exchange the stock is listed on—you actually do not even need to know. If you trade using a brokerage house, a stock trading company or an online website, all you need to have is the stock symbol of the company whose shares you want to buy or sell.

The Advantages of a Regular Investment Plan

Investing regularly and frequently skyrockets your returns

So far, the examples of compounding interest that we used were based on investing a fixed amount once and leaving it alone. I explained it this way so you could see simple examples of the benefits of the compounding curve and learn the rule of 72.

But the wise investor does not make just a one-time investment and walk away, never to invest again. The **SMART** investor keeps investing, month after month, year after year. Each time you add to your principal investment, the compounding effect increases, no matter what type of investment vehicle you choose. For example:

- Imagine that, starting today, you invest $50 per month in a savings account earning 3% for 30 years. Although you will have invested $18,000 in $50 payments for 360 months, the effect of earning compound interest will cause your investment to grow to $29,209 in 30 years.

- Even better—imagine that starting today, you invest $50 per month for the next 30 years in stocks selected from the S&P 500 Index, and assume your stocks maintain an average annual growth rate of 9.87%. If so, you would grow your money to $110,842!

In both cases, you are investing only $50/month. But where you invest that money makes an enormous difference. Would you rather have $29,000 or $110,000? I know my answer.

However, keep in mind the essential caveat of any investing: *The greater the reward, the greater the risk.* For instance, if you suddenly had to withdraw your money from the S&P 500 Index in year 15, while the stock market is in the middle of a serious downturn or even a collapse, you could end up receiving even less than the $9,000 you put in over 15 years of monthly $50 investments.

Beware of Inflation

The thief stealing your money's value

One of the basic tenets of finance is that the value of money decreases over time if it is not invested. "A dollar today is worth more than a dollar tomorrow," as the saying goes.

If you do not do anything with your money, it automatically loses value over time.

Why? The reason is **inflation,** the effect resulting from the fact that the purchasing power of money declines with passing time. We are all familiar with inflation, of course, because we experience it in our everyday lives, year after year. If you are in your 30s or over, you know that nearly everything costs more today than it did five, ten, or twenty years ago. The chart here compares the prices of items in previous years versus their average price in 2016.

	Prior Year & Average Cost	Average Cost Today
Gallon of Gasoline	1975 – $0.44	$1.90 to $3.50
New York Times Sunday Edition	1983 – $0.50	$6.00
Movie Ticket	1999 – $5.09	$8.66
Gallon of Milk	2009 – $3.05	$3.82

The rate of inflation varies each year, influenced by many economic factors, such as the employment rate, production of goods, global tensions, oil and energy prices, and other factors. All these tend to affect the purchasing power of the dollar over the course of time. When the employment rates rise, it puts pressure on salaries to rise, and this can trigger inflation. If production capacity is at its highest level, the increased demand will allow manufacturers to raise prices and trigger inflation. If oil and energy prices rise, the cost of consumer products tends to rise as well, again prompting the potential for inflation.

Inflation of the US dollar since 1915 has been a roller coaster ride, fluctuating wildly each year from a low of -10.5% in 1921 ("minus" meaning that the purchasing power of the dollar actually increased) to a high of 14.4% in 1947 (meaning that the dollar purchased nearly 15% less in 1947 than it did in 1946—a huge drop!). The chart below illustrates the inflation rate between 2005 and 2016 as an example of recent annual fluctuations. As you can see, inflation has ranged in this

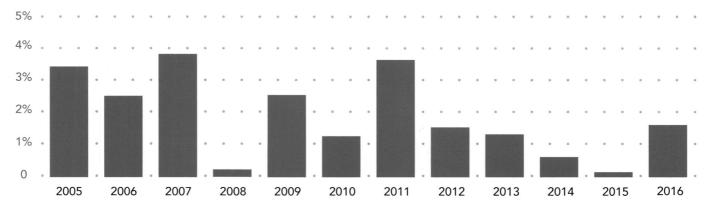

Annual Inflation Rates (2005–2016)

Inflation varies from year to year due to many factors.

ten-year period from a low near 0% to a high of about 4%.

There is an important lesson to learn about the effects of inflation on investing—*inflation can take a big bite out of your returns*. If you invest $1000 in low risk, low reward instruments, such as a bank savings account that pays only 1% interest, while the annual inflation rate is 1%, it basically means that your investment does not grow at all. You might earn $10 in interest, but the purchasing power of your $1010 after one year is still just $1000 because of inflation. And, worse, if inflation that year happens to be 2%, you will have actually lost money, as your investment's buying power would be worth only $990.

Taking inflation into account is a **SMART** reason to seek out higher yielding investment instruments that produce returns greater than the inflation rate. Inflation can be unpredictable, as the chart shows, so by seeking out high-reward investments, at least for some of your portfolio, you can stay ahead of the inflation monster.

Inflation is as violent as a mugger,
as frightening as an armed robber and
as deadly as a hit man.
—RONALD REAGAN

Our Psychological Failings

Why most investors never make money in the stock market

The objective of investing has historically been to participate wisely in *profitable* businesses and accordingly increase one's wealth to fund a better lifestyle, provide support for one's family, or participate in philanthropic goals by donating money to support good causes or to assist those in need.

However, historically most stock market investors have failed to achieve their goals for one reason: they do not understand that the stock market goes through regular cycles of ups and downs and thus fail to maximize their returns while avoiding downturns.

Major stock market declines and crashes are not a rare phenomenon. Market declines date as far back as the days of Shakespeare, when there was a sort of barter system for investors in commodities. Even that primitive market had its crashes. Every stock exchange in history has had periods of extreme downturns, sometimes as long as ten years. I call these the "lost decades."

A recent example of this phenomenon are investors who invested in the stock market in 2007, only to discover that after 8 years in 2015, they had made almost nothing! The market crash of 2008 was so severe, it wiped out all the gains investors had made in all those years. And worse, when adjusted for inflation, an investor's return was actually negative.

Huge financial losses from a lost decade have occurred numerous times over the last century. Each time one occurs, investors are shocked and disappointed, forgetting that such declines have occurred before. Many respond by pulling their money out of the stock market, just when they should probably be investing more aggressively into it.

In recent years, the threat of another market decline or crash is so worrisome that many individual and even institutional investors have become underinvested in stocks compared to their historic participation levels. In my experience,

the key is not to worry about risk, but to manage it. Done right, managing risk allows you to stay invested during great bull markets in the quest for superior returns, while minimizing losses as soon as you spot a bear market coming.

Wealth is not without its advantages and the case to the contrary, although it has often been made, has never proved widely persuasive.

—JOHN KENNETH GALBRAITH

In order not to be a disappointed stock market investor, you need to follow these three steps:

- Educate yourself in the history of markets and in economics. This knowledge is immensely important for successful investing.

- Be aware when you are reacting to your fears and greed. This reactivity tends to overrule good judgment of process and analysis.

- Take steps to ensure "risk management," i.e., protect your investments through strategic moves to minimize losses and maximize gains.

Extensive research and decades of experience in investing have taught me that the extreme losses and disappointment that come with underperforming investments can be avoided. You can learn how to avoid making bad choices in your investment instruments, and how to protect yourself against "lost decades" when your wealth barely grows or even declines. This book will teach you how to follow the three steps so you won't be a disappointed investor but rather a **SMART** one—savvy, informed, prudent, confident . . . wealthy.

The Impact of Global Forces

What happens in the world affects your money

I would be remiss in this chapter not to cover another topic of great importance to investors. The US financial markets are part of a global world today. On one hand, this means there is opportunity to invest and make a profit on literally hundreds of thousands of companies trading in every nation on the planet. In fact, half of the world's capitalization (investment in companies) is outside the US.

But the global world we live in also means that financial markets now face greater risks. As powerful and wealthy as our country is, our economy and stock markets are not isolated from the rest of the world. With advanced technologies, 24/7 communication, and the globalization of trade, it is increasingly true that financial markets worldwide are all highly connected.

This means that US investors need to be aware that there are many global forces impacting their investments. Global financial markets are inherently unstable. This is because they are sensitive to, and even anticipate, all types of changes that affect them. These include changes related to geopolitics, competition for oil and other energy products, newly emerging or declining economies, government taxation policies, advancing technologies, and even pop culture, to name a few.

Since about 2001, for example, we have seen the rapid expansion of China and Chinese products into many nations, as well as the emergence of an enormous Chinese middle class fueling a demand for consumer products and using more and more resources and energy. Other nations are also boosting their economies, particularly India (and for a while, so were Brazil and Russia, though they are now having problems.) In contrast, since 2008, economic problems caused by lagging economies and government budget deficits have affected the countries referred to as the PIGS: Portugal, Italy, Greece and Spain.

All such changes, disruptions, and alterations around the world affect the stability of US financial markets, creating periods of heightened risk and volatility. They can be mitigated either through policy or economic corrections we make in the US to calm our own markets, or they may self-correct. These disruptions usually, but not always, last just 6–12 months. A look back at history reveals periods of both long and short disruptions and losses.

JAPAN
Vast economic slowdown

BRAZIL
Rapid growth driving inflation

RUSSIA
Putting pressure on Europe over energy supplies

UNITED KINGDOM
Deciding to withdraw from the EU in Brexit vote, creating global financial turmoil

We are now, once again, in an era of significant turmoil related to geopolitics and global economic competition among many nations that seek to expand their exports around the world and to grow their middle class consumer markets.

And if international market competition were not enough to worry the financial markets, the globe also suffers from "over-leveraged" balance sheets, meaning that governments have borrowed far too much money given their financial resources and gross domestic product

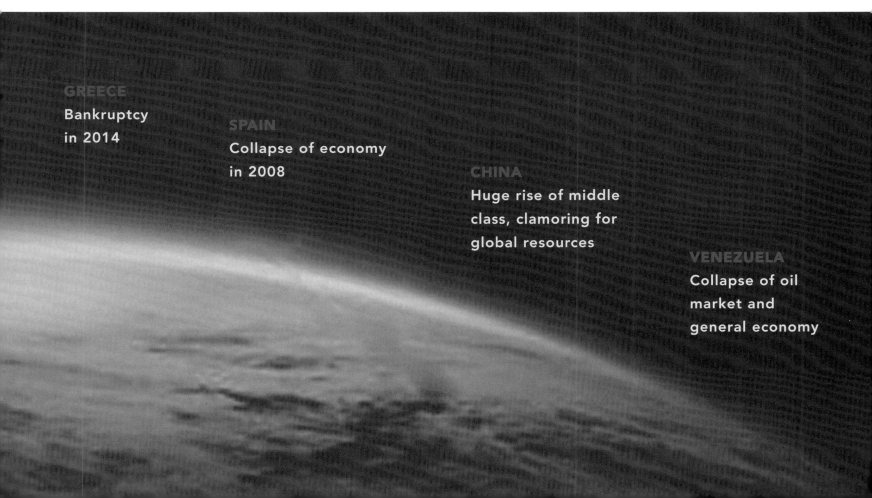

GREECE
Bankruptcy
in 2014

SPAIN
Collapse of economy
in 2008

CHINA
Huge rise of middle
class, clamoring for
global resources

VENEZUELA
Collapse of oil
market and
general economy

(GDP), particularly among the developed nations in North America and Europe. The rationale for this borrowing goes back to the crash of 2008, which jeopardized the biggest banks of the world (too big to fail, but some did!). There was little question that US federal government lending to the banks to avert yet another Great Depression was necessary in 2008.

However, the resulting US government debt burden has created major structural changes in the global economy that have led to a cascading array of negative repercussions, starting with slower economic growth, particularly in developed nations. The slower growth led to higher levels of unemployment. This then led to reduced levels of personal income growth as well

---

I'd like to live as a poor man with lots of money.
—PABLO PICASSO

---

as pockets of social unrest, such as Occupy Wall Street in the US.

All these consequences are occurring against the backdrop of a long-term economic power shift from the developed regions of the world to emerging countries such as China and India. Moreover, we are witnessing pro-democracy revolutions throughout the globe, which may be positive in the long term but create

market volatility and risk in the short term.

The aim of my book is not to explain the intricacies of these global market changes, or their causes and solutions. Rather, my goal is to lay the groundwork for how an investor like you can successfully navigate turbulent global change and its coincident heightened risk and volatility while protecting assets and achieving optimal returns to meet long-term objectives.

Changing Mindsets

The old rules of investing are no longer valid

My research suggests that this new era of higher risk and volatility may persist for some time to come. It is critical for investors to respond to this new era with a new psychology, fundamentally changing the manner by which they set their objectives for growth and, equally important, the very process by which they invest.

Both the former, solidly-held belief in "buy and hold" and the once popular "modern portfolio theory" have not worked in the past decade. Neither strategy will work in the foreseeable future because of the radical global changes in the markets. The typical investor's obsession with quick returns, especially common during past bull markets, must be abandoned.

The financial markets are not what they were as recently as a decade ago. We are living in a volatile new world, but there are still vast opportunities for disciplined investors who are willing to change their mindset, abandon the investing beliefs of before, and embrace a new era.

I call the years between 2000 and 2010 "the lost decade" since the S&P 500 Index provided investors no return during this time frame. This financial chasm ruined the dreams of many baby boomers who had expected to grow their assets for retirement and institutional investors who needed to grow their endowment to meet predetermined spending policies. I hope this book provides you with the most useful tools to successfully generate positive total returns in line with your objectives, even during "lost decades."

CHAPTER TWO

A History *of* Global Market Volatility

STOCK MARKET BOOMS, BUSTS AND LOST DECADES

" You might say that economic history is the history of people learning to manage risk.

—*James Surowiecki* "

History Repeats Itself

Today's unstable markets are not surprising

IN THE PRIOR CHAPTER, WE SAW THAT investing in the market can cause one to go though "lost decades"—periods of time when your money earns absolutely nothing—or even declines in value. While financial investing can

provide great results, it can also terrorize. When bubbles burst and markets crash, the future life plans of investors can be completely destroyed.

Crisis times are not new to finance, but most investors do not know or recall this. Tumbling valuations and lost years are not just a 21st century phenomenon. Ever since the equivalent of the modern day stock market was invented in Amsterdam in 1602, there have been scores of major crises. In former times, they were literally called "panics"—and they often wiped away investors' entire savings, demolishing dreams of wealth and financial independence. Each of these panics may have been fueled by economic factors, but they usually involved a certain amount of fear and greed that acted like tinder to ignite the market into a fireball of chaos, leading to many lost years of declining value. Here are nine of the biggest panics that are notable for how they originated and spread.

1825

CALLED THE "PANIC OF 1825," IT IS
considered the first modern stock market crash.
It originated from the Bank of England which had
made risky investments in Latin American countries (including investing in a fake country that one
Englishman had invented). After the investments
skyrocketed in value due to speculation, they suddenly collapsed (of course!). Scores of small English
banks were forced to close and many people lost
money they had invested in the market bubble.

1857

CONSIDERED THE FIRST REAL GLOBAL
financial crisis, this panic began in the US following the period of great prosperity in the early
1850s. In 1857, the market for US-made goods
declined in Europe, causing an economic downturn in America. The migration of settlers to the
western part of the US by train also slowed,
causing a decline in railroad company stocks.
Unemployment rose, the stock market declined,
farmers lost their investments, and eventually the
panic spread to banks worldwide. The market
did not recover until the end of the Civil War.

1907

CALLED THE 1907 BANKER'S PANIC, THIS
crisis began when the New York Stock Exchange
collapsed by almost 50% in just three weeks from
its previous high. The US was already in a recession, so the market crash had further cascading
effects on the entire economy. Additionally, an in-
side scheme to corner the stock market on United
Copper Company fell through, and many banks
that had purchased stocks went bankrupt. All
combined, the public panicked that year, and with-
drew money from their regional bank accounts *en
masse*. Many businesses also went bankrupt. The

situation calmed only due to an infusion of capital from JP Morgan himself. This panic led to the creation of the Federal Reserve System, the first central bank in the US, in an effort to gain better control over the banking system and the markets.

1929

OCTOBER 28 AND 29, 1929, KNOWN AS Black Monday and Black Tuesday, are considered the actual start dates of The Great Depression, the worst economic collapse in world history. On those two days alone, the DOW stock market index fell 25%, already following several prior declines of more than 10% in the month before. Throughout the 1920s, the stock market had risen on waves of investor optimism and speculative ventures, but investors got cleaned out on Black Monday and Black Tuesday, and their investments had almost no value. Over the next year, the US economic collapse spread throughout the world. In every country, personal incomes declined precipitously, prices dropped, and national economies stalled. Unemployment in the US rose to a whopping 25%, and in some countries it went as high as 33%. The

Great Depression is generally considered to have ended only thanks to the start of World War II, especially in 1941 when the US began mobilizing its economy to help the Allies. The market then took decades to recover. In fact, the US stock market did not reach its former high of Sept 3, 1929 until November 23, 1954.

1962

THE STOCK MARKET DID WELL FROM THE 1940s up until this time. The US economy was booming and stocks reflected the general optimism. But there remained an undercurrent of fear that 1929 could happen again. Many investors were betting on a bear market to come soon. Just as President John F. Kennedy took office in early 1962, the market began a sharp descent, with the S&P declining 22.5% over several short months (including a 40% drop on a single scary day in May alone). It did not recover until after the Cuban Missile Crisis in October of that year. The panic is known as the Kennedy Slide of 1962 or the Flash Crash. It is largely attributed to a market "correction" mixed with irrational consumer fears that drove the correction far too low.

1973 _through_ 1987

1973 through 1974

ON THE HEELS OF A VERY GOOD 1972, this panic was an almost two-year bear market that began in January 1973 and went all the way through December 1974. It impacted nearly every major stock market throughout the world. In the US, the Dow Jones Industrial Average lost almost 45% of its market value in that timeframe. The bear market is blamed on the collapse of the Bretton Woods system of international monetary management that most Western nations had agreed to, using gold and the US dollar as standards of currency value to avoid international financial competition (such as when a nation devalued its currency to make its goods cheaper for export). The crash especially affected the London Stock Exchange's FT 30 Index, which lost 73% of its value. The US market did not return to the December 1974 level until many years later.

1987

IN AUGUST, THE MARKETS PEAKED BUT then started to decline through September and October. Suddenly, on October 19th, the Dow fell a whopping 22.6% on a single day—making it down 36.7% from its high in August. The crash was blamed on stocks being overvalued, but also on jittery investors wanting to sell at the same time.

2002

THIS CRASH IS OFTEN REFERRED TO AS the "Internet bubble," when, following the tragedy of September 11, 2001, the markets recovered on rising optimism that internet and technology companies would enrich many investors. This hope reflected a highly bullish market throughout most of the 1990s under President Bill Clinton, when the market was rising about 15% per year between 1995 and 2000. In 2002, the bottom fell out of the technology market and the prior large gains were nearly wiped out in the coming months through October 2002. In effect, the S&P 500 lost 50% since its highs of 2000 and the NASDAQ was down nearly 80% from its high in 2000. Yikes!

2007 *through* 2008

REFERRED TO AS THE GREAT RECESSION, this recent economic panic came closest to being another Great Depression. The US National Bureau of Economic Research officially states that the recession started in December 2007 and ended in June 2009, but many economists consider that the economic slowdown and hardship continued for several more years, even through 2012 with ongoing high levels of unemployment, a lack of consumer confidence, lower consumer consumption, inflation, and many business and personal bankruptcies. As with other panics, the years prior to this stock market collapse had been full of optimistic speculation and rising stock values, creating a bubble. Another cause often cited for the Great Recession was the collapse of the "subprime" mortgage market, in which millions of mortgages were oversold by unscrupulous bankers to people speculating on fast-rising home values. When the housing boom suddenly burst in 2007, millions of homeowners could not pay their mortgages, and the risky subprime mortgages became worthless. Many banks failed or came close to bankruptcy, and some banks were bailed out by loans from the US government. Following major losses in the stock market, the US economy slowed to a crawl, and a ripple effect spread across financial markets throughout the world.

The Silver Lining in Economic and Stock Market Cycles

Some good comes out of them

The response to financial crises has long followed a familiar pattern. It starts with blame, as something or someone in the financial system is vilified: a poorly managed bank, a rogue investor, or a bad financial instrument is identified as the culprit and is then banned or regulated out of existence. Meanwhile, other elements of the financial system that are deemed essential are given more scrutiny, a few new laws are then made and new agencies created . . . but the system largely goes back to business as usual. This is the approach that seems most sensible and reassuring to the public, who want to believe in the free market. Average investors want to feel that the choice to invest as they see fit should always win out over a too-highly regulated market.

But these panics have indeed led to a silver lining of small, incremental improvements in the financial market system, including tighter regulations and more protections for consumers. The various crises over the past 200 years have helped create many new financial institutions—the New York Stock Exchange, the Federal Reserve System, the Federal Deposit Insurance Corporation, and several giant US and British banks, all of which have their roots in attempts to make the financial markets more stable, efficient, and friendly to investors.

Keep in mind that these improvements were not the products of careful design in calm times. They were cobbled together to act as safety nets at the bottom of cliffs. What often started as a simple post-crisis fix became a permanent feature of the system. That explains why many institutions and regulations in place today are still imperfect, and the public cannot be assured that another major upheaval or crash won't occur.

No matter how many fixes are applied, there will be more boom and bust cycles and more lost decades. Investors, beware.

Investor Psychology Magnifies Immediate Booms and Busts

Humans can be pretty crazy about stocks . . . when prices are going up . . . or down!

While the "boom" and "bust" cycles of the market may have their origins in economic trends and events, there is no doubt they can be temporarily magnified by investor psychology. The more markets advance, earning profits for those who are in it, the more new investors want to participate. Since investors are human, and often let greed take over rational thinking, they tend to invest when markets appear safe and are moving upwards, which is usually after prices have risen for a number of years.

With more people investing, competition increases, driving stock prices ever higher and higher . . . until eventually they become inflated beyond reasonable value. Investor fears that prices have climbed too high then set in, motivating many people to sell their stocks. In the worst cases, the downward momentum turns into a free-for-all sell-off, leading to a market crash or a prolonged period of decline (a "bear" market). In this way, investor psychology can be a significant contributing factor to intensify both market booms and busts in the short term.

PRINCIPLE 4
BEWARE OF THE CROWD EFFECT

Whenever you hear news about the stock market—whether it's skyrocketing up or tumbling down—be sure to ask yourself whether the trend is based on fact or investor psychology going haywire. Many blips on the stock market radar screen are simply due to a momentary sense of greed or fear among investors. No matter if it is a record-setting up day or a terrifying down day on Wall Street, it doesn't mean you should necessarily do something.

Stock Market Cycles Are Continuously Repetitive!

More than you might imagine

The panics and boom and bust cycles of the stock market seem to occur willy-nilly, making them difficult to predict. However, the good news is that, while the market's up and downs are largely unpredictable, they are repetitive. This means that there is a certain detectable pattern of cycles that repeat themselves somewhat regularly.

In fact, the history of the stock market shows that peaks and valleys occur about every seven to nine years, though some variation exists in certain decades when the cycle is as frequent as five years, or as infrequent as nine years.

Peaks are formed when stocks rise dramatically, due to factors like consumer confidence,

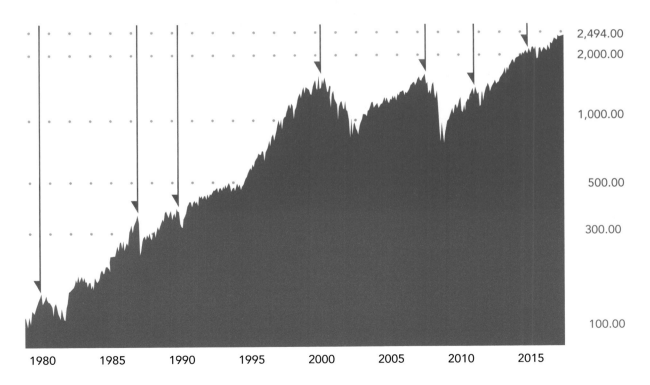

low inflation, and expanding markets. During these times, astute investors are able to profit from the increase in value and garner tremendous returns on their investment.

Valleys occur when a combination of factors such as national and global economic conditions and investor psychology coalesce to force a sharp downward trend in stock values and returns.

Being knowledgeable about what leads up to these cycles is invaluable for today's investor. With a better perspective on this repetitive cycle of advances and declines, you can adapt to it. This knowledge is what helps you understand why your goal should be to capture the benefits of the upside while avoiding the negative effects of getting caught in significant declines.

How many millionaires do you know who have
become wealthy by investing in savings accounts?
I rest my case.
—ROBERT G. ALLEN

Bull and Bear Markets

You've probably heard the terms "bull market" and "bear market." Where did they come from?

One theory is that the metaphors were chosen based on the way these animals swipe at their opponents. A bull thrusts its horns up into the air while a bear swipes its paws down.

Another theory is that a bull charges forward, while a bear slumbers.

Either way, bull markets head upwards, while bear markets head downwards. Bull market periods have rapid growth because investors are optimistic, confident and have good expectations that market values will rise. Bear markets are slowdowns, because investors are pessimistic, lack confidence and believe the market will have weak results.

The Nature of Uncertainty—Two Types of Risk

The kind you know, and the kind you don't know

Despite the ability to recognize the pattern of stock market cycles, it is important to stress that investing still remains an uncertain game . . . and that uncertainty creates risk. No one, not even a genie who can peer into a crystal ball and see the future, is able to assess with accuracy when a market bubble will suddenly take shape, gracing investors with rising stock prices and juicy profits—but neither can anyone predict when that bubble might pop, draining away profits and deflating the dreams of investors.

In the book, *Global Perspectives on Investment Management*, Peter Bernstein deftly captures the predicament:

> *Investing is unlike many other fields of endeavor because uncertainty is lodged in its heart. When we think we know the future, we are setting ourselves up for trouble. Trends are not destiny. We are no more able to extend smooth lines into the future than a sailor can observe what lies ahead on a choppy sea.*

It is important to understand that there are two types of risk. The first type are those we can know about and measure—such as the risk of getting snow on January 15 in Iowa, or the risk of a product made of .001 cm plastic ripping. We can estimate these risks based on past data, and make approximations of the uncertainty happening. What's great news is that financial models have been invented to estimate this type of uncertainty and risk in the stock market—models like probability analysis, normal curve sampling, regression analysis, and other fancy mathematical and statistical concepts that can be enormously helpful in making financial uncertainty seem less uncertain.

The second type of risks, however, are those we cannot know or measure. This unknown encompasses vast, unchartered territory—a place where we do not know what we do not know. It is this degree of unknown that creates an element of *true risk*. As a result of this second type of risk, there are times when our decisions, even those taken with all knowable risks in mind, will simply be the wrong ones.

Given this truth, risk management is not just about calculating potential risk scenarios. It is also about learning how to make quality decisions in the face of unknowable uncertainty and recognizing that decisions may be impossible to get right. But as a **SMART** investor, one must be prepared for the unknowable future to ensure you do not experience the worst consequences. You need to put processes in place and use the tools at your disposal to protect your investments against the vagaries of the unknown future.

Investing is a Competitive Sport

To make money, you have to want to win

I'm sure that when you were a child playing a game or a sport, you preferred winning over losing. There's something in our psychological makeup that makes us competitive, whether we're competing against other people, against the clock, or against a set of rules such as in a game of solitaire (where you can't cheat, at least not on a computer). In recent years, some psychologists have tried to convince parents that it is unimportant, even deleterious to one's character, for children to compete. In their view, children should learn that non-competition, teamwork, cooperation, and collaboration are the keys to success as adults.

However, the financial markets have no such tolerance for the lack of a competitive spirit in investors. If you intend to invest, you must be aware that millions of other investors are competing against you for the monetary gains that investing can achieve. Like you, they want to make the best choices possible for their investments, and to grow their assets to the highest levels possible. They, or their financial advisors, are buying and selling financial instruments—such as stocks, bonds, mutual funds, and ETFs—in competition with you. When you seek to buy, someone else seeks to sell at a profit. When you want to sell, there's a buyer who wants to have it at the lowest price possible.

To put it bluntly, investing is a competitive sport . . . and you cannot play it unless you want to win. You need to be willing to learn the rules so you can play the game well. You need to know how to deal with the uncertainty of the market and to take calculated **SMART** risks that minimize the number of wrong decisions you might make, while maximizing the number of right decisions you make, even in the face of an unknowable future.

Just as in sports, business (or love), competing can be stressful. Whether you invest on your own or hire a financial advisor, you might worry about losing part or all of your investment. Some investors worry so much that they spend hours every day watching the market and trying to second guess its movements. They may trade more frequently than they need to, or make brash and hasty decisions that turn out to be worse than having left their money invested where it originally was.

If you are familiar with the Great Depression of 1929, which lasted until about 1939, you undoubtedly know about the deep psychological scars that this lost decade left on millions of families who saw their entire life savings, their homes, and their dignity vanish with the market crash. Photos of desperate, sad-eyed men lining up by the hundreds to find some work and families waiting in soup lines reflect many bleak years of lost hope and broken lives.

The 'Ugly Math' of Recouping Losses

Gotta make up for what you lost before you get even

When the market goes through its down cycles, it is not only psychologically difficult on investors, but also financially devastating. The loss of value in investments during a downward trend creates what I call "ugly math."

First, market cycles that engender wide swings can completely void the rule of 72 regarding how long it takes to double your money. If an investor happens to enter the market at the exact moment when the market has peaked and is commencing a steep downward trend that lasts four, five, or six years, the returns will drop precipitously. Steep valleys are precisely why investors sometimes end up with a lost decade, when their assets gain nothing or lose value.

Secondly, even short-term market declines can have a significant impact on investors. This is one of the most misunderstood concepts in the investment field today. The math of recovering from substantial losses is ugly and gets uglier as the percentage of loss increases. Any time

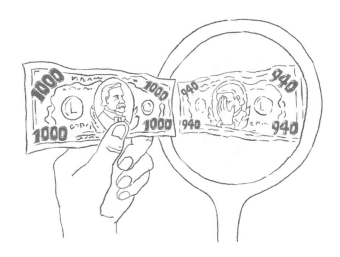

your investments lose value, it creates a situation that I call "ugly math."

This is because any loss in portfolio value requires a much bigger percentage gain to fully recover the original portfolio value. For example, let's say an investor purchased stocks for $10,000. In the first year, the portfolio declines 35%. Following that, the portfolio increased an average of 9% per year.

This is where the ugly math comes in. When the portfolio declined by 35%, it reduced the investor's nest egg to just over $6,000. Even if the portfolio recovers at 9% per year, it takes six years to come back to the original market value of $10,000, as the chart below shows. In effect, the investor must regain not 35% but 54% to get even with the original investment.

Significant declines are thus hard to recover from in terms of both time and the need to

Ugly Math

A 35% PORTFOLIO DECLINE REQUIRES A 54% ADVANCE! . . . AND A LOT OF YEARS

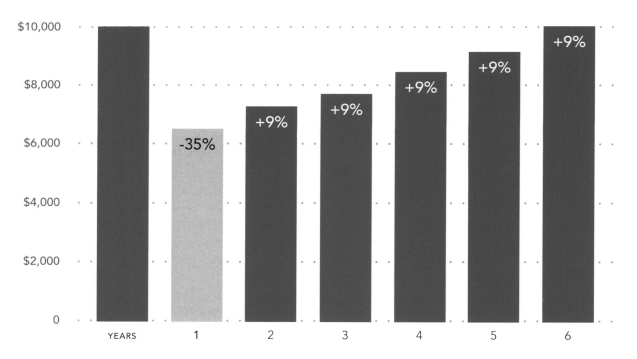

The "ugly math" of losses suggests that it can take a very long time to recoup your original investment if there is a sharp fall in the stock market. Here, a 35% portfolio decline at the end of year 1 requires 6 years to recoup the loss, even if the portfolio earns an average of 9% per year in rebounding.

achieve larger returns. The greater the loss, the worse this ugly math becomes. In 2008 when global markets declined more than 50%, investors who didn't manage this risk had to increase their portfolios an unimaginable 100% to get even. No wonder it took seven years for the market to return to its pre-2008 levels.

The concept of ugly math is critical to successful investing and meeting your long-term goals. It is a concept that highlights the relationship between time and money. We only have so much time to invest towards our goals. Sustaining large losses forces investors to postpone their financial goals and in some cases destroys them altogether.

In other words, any loss, even a short-term one, can be very destructive to investors. Recapturing your value requires the market to surge beyond the percentage of loss incurred just to return to your starting point.

The chart on the next page shows the percentage increase required to recover from various losses. This chart makes it clear that recovering from a large loss requires much more significant returns than most investors realize or may be willing to risk. For example, a $1,000,000 portfolio that declines 50% translates to a portfolio value of $500,000 and a loss of $500,000. (Wow, that feels terrible, and how would you explain that to your spouse, board members or trust beneficiaries, who believed you were investing wisely?) But more importantly, this degree of loss requires a 100% gain to recover the original portfolio value: $500,000 + 100% = $1,000,000. However, to realize 100% portfolio appreciation can take many, many years.

PRINCIPLE 5

THE STOCK MARKET IS A JUNGLE

The stock market crash of 2008 was a brutal reminder of the ordeals that families experienced during the Great Depression. The Great Recession has served as a stark warning to many people that investing is not a game. It cannot be approached with whimsy or ignorance. The market is like a jungle, a very sophisticated, complex, and unpredictable place to put your money . . . and all precautions must be taken to ensure that you compete knowledgeably and come out a winner.

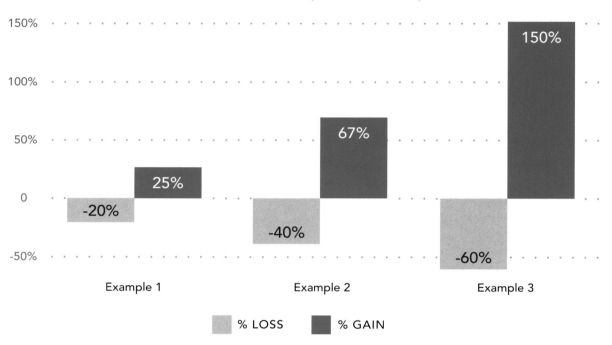

% Investment Gain Required to Recoup Loss

The "ugly math" of stock market losses shows how you need to recoup 25% after a 20% decline, 67% after a 40% decline, and 150% after a 60% decline to come back to your original investment amount.

Return, Risk and Volatility

Over 89 years (beginning in 1928 and ending in 2016), the US stock market (as measured by the S&P 500 Index) produced a compound annual return of 9.5%. But the market can be volatile, too. On occasion the S&P 500 Stock Index has experienced advances or declines of up to 50% within two years. Numerous declines of various percentages have occasionally marred upticks. And keep in mind that, after the "Great Depression," the bursting of the internet bubble in 2000, and the "Great Recession" of 2008, investors have had to wait at least 7 years for their portfolio to return to its earlier value.

Stock Market Annual End-of-Year Results
Over 89 Years (1928–2016)

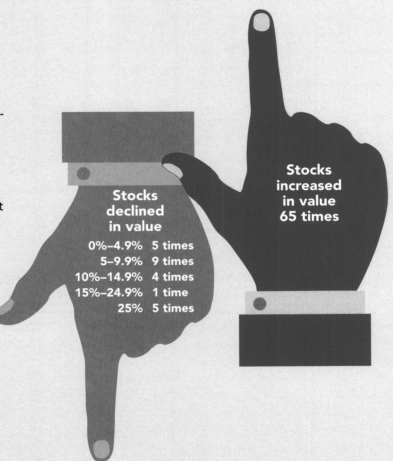

Stocks declined in value

0%–4.9%	5 times
5–9.9%	9 times
10%–14.9%	4 times
15%–24.9%	1 time
25%	5 times

Stocks increased in value 65 times

Even Uglier Math for Retirees

Withdrawals in a down market are like compound interest in reverse!

In addition to the loss of growth in value or income in a down period or during a slow recovery, the math gets even uglier when investors need to make withdrawals during that time to have cash to live on. This is the often the case for retirees who need the money from their investments each month. Each time they withdraw, they reduce their capital base. This is a "double whammy" for retired people. The effect of taking capital away from their portfolio while it is in a downward trend or in recovery mode adds tremendous pressure on the percentage of market increase required to attain the full recapture of their original investment amount. When retirees get stuck in a lost decade or even a bad short-term market downturn, the impact on their assets can be devastating. It's like the power of compounding interest—but in reverse!

This graphic illustrates the dilemma for retirees. Here, a $10,000 investment that loses 35% in the first year of a bear market will take 15 years to recoup the initial investment even when regaining 9% per year if a retiree is taking out 4% per year.

This type of situation creates the possibility that some people lose so much of their savings that they outlive their assets in retirement—a very big risk for millions of older investors today! This is where the connection between time and money becomes clear and should be a primary consideration for an investor.

PRINCIPLE 6

YOU MUST AVOID THE BULK OF DECLINES

The goal in SMART investing is to mitigate the potential for catastrophic losses from market downturns, and instead capitalize on market upturns! Though it is impossible to know exactly when markets will begin a downward descent, or when they will hit bottom, with research and good advice, one can miss the bulk of a devastating decline. If you avoid most of the time that markets are declining, you will be far ahead of the game, because you have much less catching up to do. You need not predict either the top or the bottom with precision—just be savvy enough to avoid the bulk of the decline. This will allow you to retain most of your capital, which will compound your wealth significantly every time the market recovers.

Even Uglier Math For Retirees

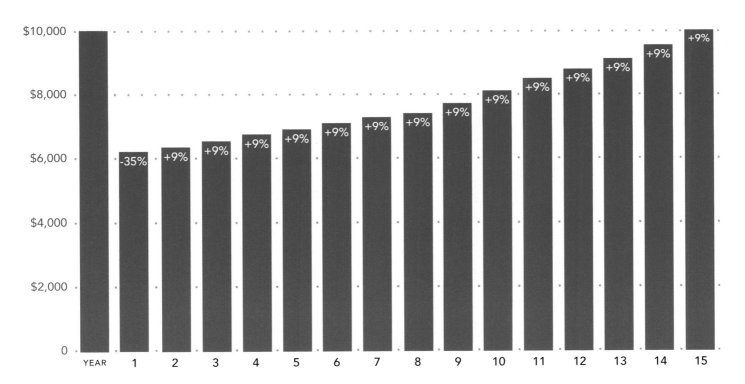

	YEAR	1	2	3	4	5	6	7	8	9	10	11	12	13	14	15
		-35%	+9%	+9%	+9%	+9%	+9%	+9%	+9%	+9%	+9%	+9%	+9%	+9%	+9%	+9%

The "ugly math" is even uglier for retirees who are withdrawing money from their investment to live on each year. For example, a decline of 35% on an investment of $10,000 will take 15 years to recover, even when rebounding at 9% per year if a retiree is withdrawing 4% ($400) per year.

How the Stock Market Has Fared Across the Decades

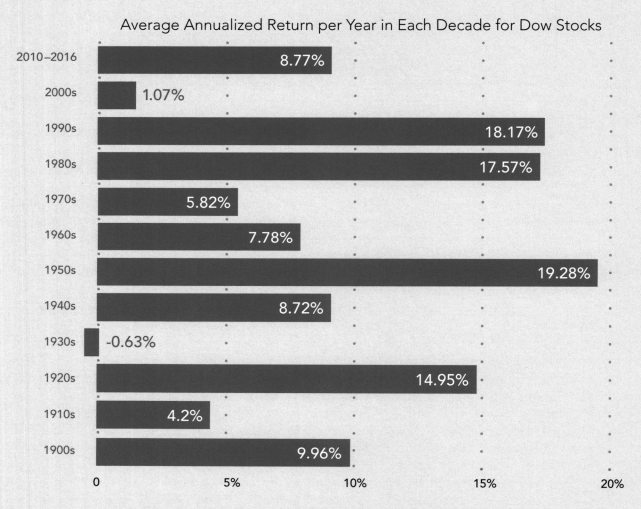

Average Annualized Return per Year in Each Decade for Dow Stocks

Decade	Return
2010–2016	8.77%
2000s	1.07%
1990s	18.17%
1980s	17.57%
1970s	5.82%
1960s	7.78%
1950s	19.28%
1940s	8.72%
1930s	-0.63%
1920s	14.95%
1910s	4.2%
1900s	9.96%

The chart shows the range of experiences a long-term investor might have in the stock market. As you can see, there are the "great decades, "so-so decades," and "lost decades." The stock market can be volatile from decade to decade. Although many decades produce 10% to nearly 20% average annual returns, several result in only 4% to 9% returns—and two are "lost decades" with nearly no return or a negative return.

Doubling Your Money in the Stock Market

History tells us how long it takes

The discussion above raises the question: how long does it usually take to double your money if you invest in the stock market? Statisticians are able to answer this question quite precisely: Over its long history of more than 100 years, the stock market has yielded an average annual return between 8% and 9.5%. This would suggest that, according to the rule of 72, you can double your money in the stock market in roughly 8 to 10 years. However, you would have to pick the right 8– to 10–year period when the market is generally rising—not a lost decade.

WARNING

There are Many Ways to Evaluate Stock Market Returns

You have to ask which way is being used

When you see charts like the one on the previous page, you have to find out what method was used to calculate the returns. There are three factors to take into account if you want to truly know the "real" annualized rate of return in the stock market.

Simple vs. Compound Growth Rate

First, you must determine if the calculations were done according to the "simple" growth rate or the "compound" annual growth rate.

The difference between the two is important. For example, let's say you invested $1,000 in the stock market. In the first year, it grew 100% to $2,000, but in the second year, it lost 50% of its value, returning you back to your $1,000 initial investment. The simple growth rate, based on the arithmetic mean, is 25% (derived from 100%-50% = 50% divided by 2 years = 25%).

Of course, this number is meaningless in clarifying your growth rate, because you are actually back down to zero return.

It is therefore more useful to calculate returns based on the compound annual growth rate (often abbreviated as CAGR), which is determined using a complex formula:

$$(1 + r_{ave})^2 - StdDev^2 = (1 + CAGR)^2$$

You do not need to know this formula, of course, but if you have the opportunity to work with a financial advisor, or if you explore calculators on the Internet, you can learn the compound annual growth rate of your investment in the stock market. This can be invaluable, because the CAGR more accurately reflects the impact of market declines on your rate of return.

The Effect of Dividends on Rate of Return

When calculating your rate of return in the stock market, you also need to consider whether any of the stocks you own have paid dividends. If you were to try to assess your return on investment based solely on the difference between the purchase price of a stock and the price you sold it, you would only be evaluating the stock's appreciation (rise in value).

For example, if you bought a stock for $100/ per share and sold it for $109/ per share a year later, you might think your gain is 9%. But what if that stock also paid a dividend of $2/ per share that year? If so, your gain is actually 11%. Of course, if you reinvest that dividend to purchase more of that same stock, it adds to the asset base used to determine the growth rate in the following year.

The approximate percentage 9.4% which is often cited as the average stock market return over the past 100 or so years includes both appreciation and dividends.

Rate of Inflation

A third factor that you must take into account in assessing your returns with stocks is the rate of inflation. As discussed earlier, inflation takes a toll on your investments. For example, an investment of $10,000 that has a 6% return and yields $10,600 in a year in which inflation is 1%, actually has an inflation-adjusted return of 4.94%. Do the math: $10,600, after 1% inflation, is worth only $10,494.

Calculating Rate of Return in the Stock Market with all 3 Factors

These three factors can substantially alter the number you get when you seek to calculate the return on investing in the stock market. For example, let's say you invested $10,000 in Standard & Poor's (S&P) 500 stocks in 1992. Here are six different ways in which one might state the return when it accounts for all the possible factors:

Measurement Used	Return	How much is $10,000 worth after 25 years (1992–2016)
1. Average Annual Rate of Return	8.9%	$84,275
2. Average Annual Rate of Return with Dividends	11.29%	$145,011
3. Average Annual Rate of Return with Dividends, Adjusted for Inflation	8.56%	$77,937
4. Compound Annual Growth Rate (CAGR)	7.3%	$58,209
5. CAGR with Dividends	9.63%	$96,300
6. CAGR with Dividends, Adjusted for Inflation	6.94%	$53,518

Annualized returns can be calculated in many ways. Any time you are quoted an annual return, you need to know what factors are being taken into account to calculate that return.

So if you ever hear anyone tell you how much they earned in the market, you need to ask if it is based on simple or compound interest, if it includes or excludes dividends, and if it is adjusted for inflation.

The Effect of Layered Fees

You also need to take into account the effect of paying "layered" fees. Investors should be on guard of excessive fees. Although a 1% fee is traditional for asset management, many managers add mutual funds and ETFs that can make the overall fee much higher and drag down performance. The graphic below shows you the impact of fees on the growth of an investment.

The Effect of Fees on Performance

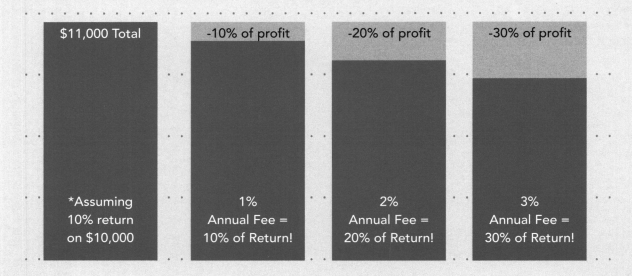

$11,000 Total	-10% of profit	-20% of profit	-30% of profit
*Assuming 10% return on $10,000	1% Annual Fee = 10% of Return!	2% Annual Fee = 20% of Return!	3% Annual Fee = 30% of Return!

Layered fees can take a substantial bite out of your returns.

These bars show how much disappears from a 10% annual return for 1%, 2% and 3% fees.

Is the Market Going Up or Down?

Good question!

After reading this chapter, you must be wondering whether the market today will climb higher—or is approaching a peak that will lead us into a valley of market losses in the coming years.

Unfortunately, no one can answer this question with absolute certainty. As I mentioned, even the fortune teller's crystal ball cannot predict what will happen in the coming years.

However, I am constantly researching, tracking, and examining many factors and indicators that help me understand market cycles and make **SMART** decisions about where I can best invest. In the following chapters, I explain the tools, rules and analysis that I use to manage return and risk in these volatile times.

CHAPTER THREE

Determining Your Personal Rate *of* Return (ROR)

HOW MUCH DO YOU REALLY NEED TO LIVE ON EACH YEAR FOR YOUR LIFESTYLE?

> An investor without investment objectives is like a traveler without a destination.
>
> —*Ralph Seger*

YOU NOW KNOW THE BASICS OF INVESTING. I have covered these topics: the instruments of investment, the notion of simple vs. compound interest, the rule of 72, the two types of risk, and the basics of the stock market and its historical volatility.

With this foundation, you are now ready to begin planning your own strategy to build wealth. In this chapter, we will explore a four-step wealth management planning process that I use. These steps reflect a belief that each person is a unique individual. Every investor deserves to have a completely personalized and customized wealth-building and wealth-preserving plan tailored to his or her lifestyle, life goals, and family circumstances.

PRINCIPLE 7
EVERYONE NEEDS AN ROR

ROR stands for Rate of Return. Any investment provides return, but also risk. The question is, how much return do you require and how much risk must you take to generate that return? In planning a strategic wealth building plan, you have to begin by understanding how much wealth will get you to your ultimate financial goal. This in turn will determine the amount of risk you need to "get there." My four-step planning process helps precisely identify your lifestyle goals for building overall wealth, immediate and regular needs for cash flow, your risk tolerance and preferences for investing, and your long-range goals for donating to charities and/or leaving an inheritance for your heirs.

STEP I. *Setting Reasonable Objectives and Goals for Your Wealth*
Calculating your needs so you don't run out of money!

The first step to building wealth is to be completely honest and objective in asking yourself the fundamental question of investing: *How much money do I really need in my lifetime?*

The answer to this question goes to the core of your being. It involves examining a wide range of factors in your life and making some calculations to create meaningful and reasonable goals for growing your wealth. The prompts below reflect the types of factors you want to consider:

- How do I want to live? What type of home do I want? What does it cost yearly to inhabit that home?

- How long do I want to work?

- What lifestyle do I want to have in terms of the luxuries I can afford—e.g., eating out, traveling, entertaining guests, spending money on myself and my family?

- How much do I need to take care of myself and my family over the long term for our health, security, and well-being?

- What charities and/or political and social causes do I want to support?

- How do I want to live in my senior years when I am no longer active? What housing and type of long-term care might I need for myself, my spouse or significant other?

- Will I be using all or some of the income derived from my investments, or will I re-invest it back into my principal to grow the amount on which I will eventually retire?

- What endowment or inheritance do I want to leave my heirs? Do I seek to set them up so that they will never need to work?

- What do I need to teach my heirs about protecting the wealth that I have built for them?

At some point in the near future, sit down and reflect on these questions. This is a first step in assessing your personal goals. Write down your estimates to assess your goals in building wealth. Be sure to put concrete dollar amounts down in answer to each question.

Note that some questions are focused on calculating annual budgetary needs—having the money you want to live on day by day for each year. Other questions are related to calculating the principal amount you want to have at the end of your life. Both of these answers are necessary to calculate the total wealth you will need to ensure you have enough money to survive and thrive each day of your life, as well as to have a residual amount to leave your heirs and/or to charities. If you were to calculate only what you need to live on during your own lifetime, and you were to then draw down that amount from your principal each year, you might end up with nothing to leave your heirs.

The biggest risk most investors face is not ending up with zero to leave their heirs, but running out of funds for themselves. This is what I call "premature financial demise," (PFD) when people do not have enough assets to continue living in the manner they are accustomed to when they are in their last and final years.

PFD can happen to even the wealthiest individuals. Stories abound of entertainment celebrities and sports stars who were once multi-millionaires, yet managed to lose their wealth to the point of needing to sell their homes and live in sparse conditions.

Therefore, as you consider your goals and needs, base your answers on a positive yet realistic view of your lifestyle and your wealth-building dreams. If you are currently living on $500,000 per year and are accustomed to traveling often, dining well, entertaining lavishly, and donating to charities, then complete your estimates to sustain that lifestyle as your goal. But it would be unrealistic to project building your wealth through investing alone such that you could live on $1,000,000 per year. Similarly, if you are currently living on $150,000 per year, complete your estimate to live on that amount, not on $300,000 per year obtained just from investing.

Let's look at some examples of how two investors think about their futures.

INVESTOR A

This investor maintains a home that he purchased for $1.2 million, with a mortgage of $800,000 that costs him $4500 per month for the next 18 years. Age 42 today, he would like to pay off his home and be free of monthly payments by the time he is 60. His income of $280,000 per year plus his wife's income of $117,000 afford them a comfortable monthly cash flow of $23,000 after taxes. The couple takes three trips per year, two of them with their two children and one of them alone to celebrate their anniversary. The trips cost the family about $45,000 per year. They donate close to $20,000 per year to charities. Investor A wants to be able to leave his children $1,000,000 each. The investor wants to sustain this lifestyle for the rest of his life, which he believes will take him into his late-80s.

INVESTOR B

This investor founded a company and sold it for $12 million. She paid cash for a home in Scottsdale, AZ, which she will bequeath to her only daughter. At age 55, she intends to continue working for another five years, if only to prevent herself from getting bored. She may try to found another company as a serial entrepreneur, but for now, she is consulting and earning $200,000 per year working only eight months. She pegs her annual future living expenses in retirement at $175,000 per year, plus she wants to leave her daughter $5,000,000. Given her family history, she feels she will live until at least until age 92 or 95.

The Long Life Conundrum

Human lifetimes have been expanding for centuries. But you may be surprised at the projections that some researchers now make about how long people might live in the near future. While the average life expectancy of an American born in 1909 was 50.23 years, by 1959 it increased to 67.55 and by 1999, it was 74.6. As the graphic below shows, it is projected that Americans, on average, could live to be 100 years old by 2030, and then to 150 years old by 2067.

The lengthening of life will be wonderful for many people, but will also bring enormous challenges to individuals and society, especially when it comes to financial needs. If the average person works for 50 years to age 70, but lives another 50 to 80 years without income from employment, where will the money come from? Depending on your age now, begin thinking about your future and how long you conceivably might be around.

Life Expectancy

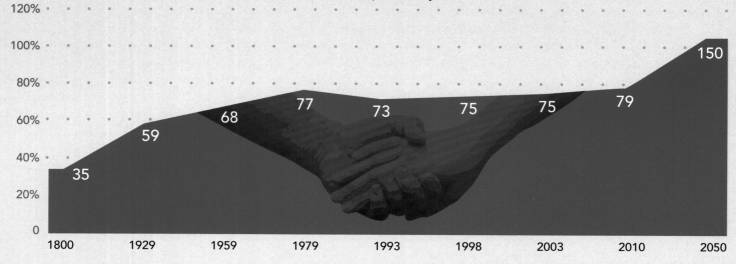

	1800	1929	1959	1979	1993	1998	2003	2010	2050
	35	59	68	77	73	75	75	79	150

Human lifetimes are expanding. It is entirely possible that people may live to 150 years old in another fifty years.

STEP 2. *Determining Your Current Assets for Investment*

How much do you have to put into the market?

You now know what your goals are for building wealth. That is your end game. The next step is to know your starting point. You can't know how to get there unless you know where you are starting from.

Assessing the value of your current assets can be simple and easy . . . or it can be complex. Depending on your current wealth, you may have bank accounts, a portfolio of stocks and bonds, cash, and other easily valued investments. If so, the job of totaling your assets may be easy enough to do on your own. You can create your own Excel spreadsheet listing your various assets, their current value, and add it up. Or you can do it by writing all your numbers down on a simple sheet of paper.

For some people, though, this step can be complicated. You may own real estate, stock options, artwork, fine wines, antique or valuable modern cars, ownership interests in businesses, and other investments that are difficult to value or take time to evaluate. You may need to employ an accountant or financial advisor to value them for you. It may take months of time

Inflation is when sitting on your nest egg doesn't give you anything to crow about.

—ANONYMOUS

to determine your current net worth with some accuracy, which is the starting point of building your future wealth.

The goal of this step is to gain an understanding of the value of all your assets, both *liquid* ones (meaning assets that are cash or can be turned into cash very quickly) and non-liquid ones. After reading this book, you may decide that you want to perform this step in order to convert some of your non-liquid assets into cash to be invested in the ways that I recommend. You might do this for non-liquid assets that are not appreciating very quickly in value. You can make more money if you convert these assets to cash and invest them in the stock market for better returns, as you will be learning in the coming chapters.

STEP 3. *Estimating the Right Rate of Return to Achieve Goals*
Finding the balance of too much vs. too little risk

The next step is calculating what level of return is required to go from Point A (your current wealth) to Point B (your goals). This can be done using a simple calculation based on a straightforward mathematical formula to estimate how much money you need to fund an "annuity"—a series of payments—that will support you during your non-working lifetime, plus leaving the residual amount you desire for your heirs.

However, this simple calculation is superficial and fails to account for the many complexities that are involved in performing a truly *strategic* portfolio planning process. You must take into account taxes, inflation, and most importantly, the risks involved in seeking a specific "rate of return," often called ROR.

As you learned in Chapter 1, there is little risk in going after a 1% return per year, while there is great risk in aiming for an 8%, 10%

or even higher annual returns. The financial markets just don't give out money at such high levels of return without investors taking risks. Each investor must therefore determine the risk they are willing to live with in order to go from their current level of wealth to the wealth they will need to fulfill their future goals and live the lifestyle they want.

How can investors determine their personal ROR and their risk tolerance? Most importantly, how can investors avoid the risk of catastrophic loss that ultimately has the potential to destroy their long-term goals?

The answer is that each investor must find their own balance between taking on too much risk to ensure they meet their goals, or too little risk to prevent loss. The risk of investing is a double-edged sword—on one side is too small a risk; on the other is too much. Each side has its drawbacks that must be weighed and balanced.

The Risk of Being Too Conservative

The mere thought of not having enough capital over time can lead investors, especially older folks who are close to retirement or already in it, to be overly cautious about their investing decisions. In the short term, this strategy can appear to be safe and psychologically comforting, based on the belief that by investing in only the most secure instruments, there is little chance of losing one's money. "Playing it safe" can be especially rationalized in a chaotic or down-trending market, especially if the investor has the responsibility of being a trustee of a trust or a board member of a finance committee for a private entity.

However, a risk-averse mindset can lead to a rate of return that is far too low for investors to make their money last the number of years they will need over the rest of their lifetime. Your nest egg can dwindle too far down in your later years, especially given how advances in healthcare are helping people stay alive for far longer than ever before. When low rates of return provide little income and one's ongoing annual expenses mount up, the math doesn't work.

If you are in your 40s, 50s, or 60s and you extrapolate a conservative plan decades into the future, the result is often a highly predictable chance that your capital will be insufficient and you will simply run out of assets sooner than your lifetime.

Let's assume an investor begins with $500,000 and it earns 7% per year. The chart below provides a visual for how quickly such an investor can draw down his or her funds over decades of time. Each line on the graph reflects the decline in the investment total given a specific rate of withdrawal.

For instance, if the investor withdraws only 5% of the total funds per year to live on (approximately $25,000 annually) we can see that the investment will last about 44 years. That might work for some people who have other money to live on, such as social security or rents from a building you own.

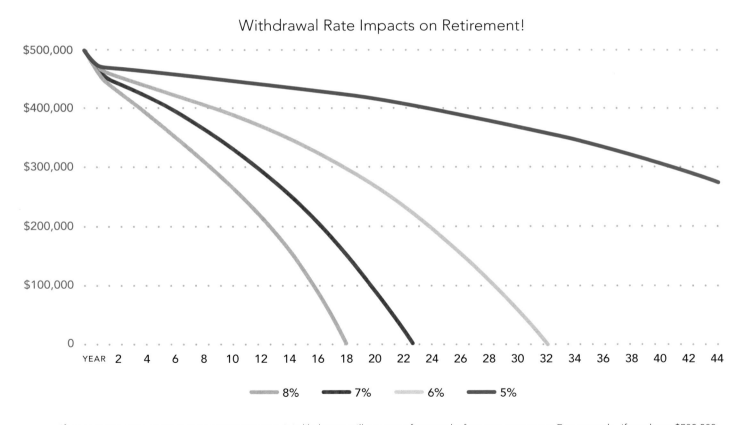

Withdrawal Rate Impacts on Retirement!

8%   7%   6%   5%

If you are too conservative in your investments, it is likely you will run out of money before you pass away. For example, if you have $500,000 and you are earning 7% per year with a 2% inflation rate, this chart shows how soon you would run out of money under various withdrawal rates.

But if the investor withdraws 8% per year to live on ($44,000 per year), even when the funds are growing by 7% per year, the total nest egg will be depleted within 18 years. If you are 65 now, you'd be broke by the time you are age 83. What if you live to age 87 or 92?

By the way, in the scenarios above, we took into account a 2% per year inflation rate because this has a serious subtractive impact on one's assets. Inflation decreases the purchasing power of money. Withdrawing $20,000 this year will purchase $20,000 of goods and services at today's value of money. But if inflation continues at about 2% per year for the next twenty years, that same $20,000 annual withdrawal will be able to purchase only $13,352 worth of goods and services at the end of that time. To keep up with the purchasing power of money, an investor has to withdraw more and more each year. We took this factor into account in projecting how long $500,000 will last at different withdrawal rates.

The Risk of Being Too Aggressive

The other side of the double-edged sword of risk is being too aggressive in one's investment strategy. Buying investment instruments such as stocks, junk bonds, Real Estate Investment Trusts (REITs), and other risky ventures that promise big payoffs can seem very attractive to an investor chasing the highest rates of return. Winning at this game can make an individual, trustee, or board member look like a genius in a rising global stock market.

However, an aggressive strategy often leads to taking ill-informed or blue sky risks, or remaining too long in a volatile market, constantly thinking that it will go up again. This is a mindset that can lead to devastating losses if the venture goes sour, or if the market for that asset suddenly takes a nosedive. This can amount to huge losses that take years to recover from.

As discussed before, history shows that many investments have taken sudden unexpected nosedives. If an aggressive investor happened to enter the stock market a month or a week before the market crashed in 1998, 2000, or 2007, he or she would have lost from 15% up to 50% of the investment over several months, and it would have taken months, if not years, to recoup those losses.

The Negative Effects of Inflation

THE FALLING VALUE OF $20,000 AT 3% INFLATION PER YEAR

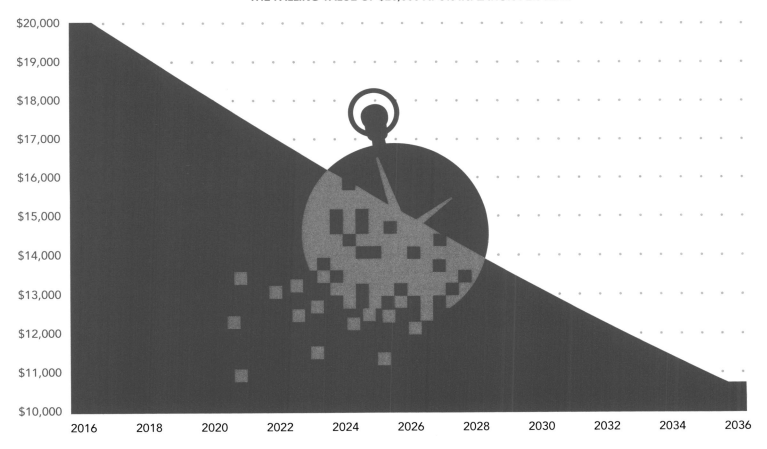

Inflation reduces the purchasing power of money. Starting in 2016, a $20,000 annual withdrawal will be able to purchase only $10,876 worth of goods and services at the end of twenty years if inflation averages 3% per year.

A Formalized Method of Determining Your ROR and Risk Levels

Modeling for 30 to 40 years

So what is the key to deciding the right ROR to achieve your goals while remaining within your risk tolerance level?

I recommend using a formal process that is essential to developing a successful portfolio of investments to match an investor's ROR needs and risk tolerance level.

This process begins with building a model using the calculations made in Step 1 to estimate current and future cash flows, plus the calculations made in Step 2 to add up all current and expected future assets and liabilities. Be sure that you have determined as accurately as possible your current assets and future expenses. Any oversight of the

usual expenses of your lifestyle and projections of knowable future one-time expenses will produce significantly skewed results over the long run that make the modeling inaccurate.

I next incorporate the data collected into a technology that projects the growth of the asset base at various ROR's over time and the corresponding cash flows that can be supported from those assets.

Using a modeling software program, I typically run the figures out 30 or 40 years because it is critical to test a long-term investment plan over this length of time. Three or four decades of projections provide a big picture perspective that ensures a person's ROR will provide enough income to support their family's lifestyle through their middle-age and senior years well into their retirement. Depending on an individual's age, the amount of time to project forward may even extend into the end of their life, thus

ensuring that they do not outlive their wealth.

This computer modeling simulates the effects of various rates of inflation on future expenses. Given that a dollar today is worth less many years in the future, the projections take into account the decreased purchasing power of future cash flows. I prefer to be conservative in this regard, using a higher than current rate of inflation to be certain that the model's projections are as accurate as possible.

Let's say that our hypothetical investor wants to take a one-month vacation every year from ages 65 to 85. The cost of twenty years of travel can be calculated using today's prices, but if inflation is not included, the figure will be far short of the amount actually needed to take nice trips. Today's $5,000 trip to Europe might cost $8,600 in five years, $12,000 in ten years, and $15,000 in twenty years. The same goes for any unique or repeating unusual expenses that the investor may want or plan on, such as giving his grandchildren a monetary gift every year, buying a new car every five years, and so on. I try to account for how inflation will affect the investor's monthly lifestyle budget as well as his or her unique expenses.

If the model is built correctly, it clearly shows how different rates of return provide different future outcomes in the life of the investor. Working backwards from how much an investor will need to fund his or her lifestyle over time, plus the desired residual wealth for heirs, I project the effects of the different rates of return on the current value of their asset base, and compare these results to what is needed. This exercise provides deep insight into the amount of required ROR so I can build an asset base through **SMART** investing that ensures the investor's portfolio meets the long-term objectives.

There are two reasons why this modeling is extremely important for individual investors and families. The first relates to age. Running out of assets at an older age is catastrophic given that one's ability to generate earned income becomes unlikely. Second, selecting the right ROR is critical for estate planning, unless the family or individual is planning on spending their last dollar on their last day. A well thought-out estate plan requires the sophisticated ROR calculation to ensure that a residual asset base remains that can be distributed to the beneficiaries in the most tax-efficient manner.

A good ROR simulation model identifies the risks of portfolio returns that are too low. It serves as a guide as to the minimum level of return necessary for investors to choose a ROR that increases their odds of maintaining a sufficient asset base to not only fund all their future expenses, but to grow in perpetuity. In a world of heightened risk and extremely volatile markets, it is better for investors to use this type of modeling to calculate their personal ROR floor. This helps them reach their goals while protecting them from the catastrophic losses that can occur from taking on too much risk.

The Unknown Risks of Inflation

Inflation takes a big bite out of your capital over long periods of time, as the chart below shows. Someone with $100,000 today will need to have the equivalent of $200,000 in 25 years! Prepare to need a lot more money in 25 years to maintain the same lifestyle you have now.

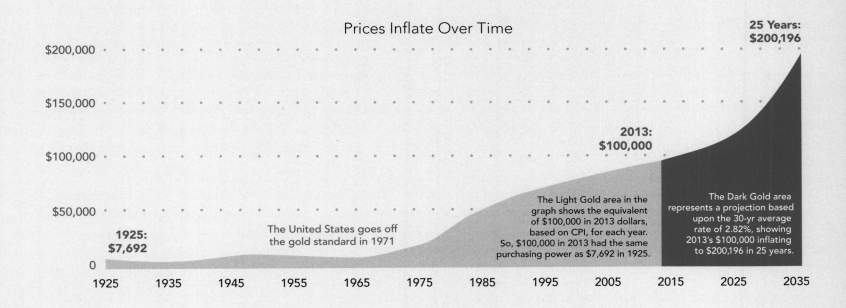

Prices Inflate Over Time

25 Years: $200,196

2013: $100,000

1925: $7,692

The United States goes off the gold standard in 1971

The Light Gold area in the graph shows the equivalent of $100,000 in 2013 dollars, based on CPI, for each year. So, $100,000 in 2013 had the same purchasing power as $7,692 in 1925.

The Dark Gold area represents a projection based upon the 30-yr average rate of 2.82%, showing 2013's $100,000 inflating to $200,196 in 25 years.

Inflation reduces the purchasing power of your money. What $7692 could buy in 1925 costs $100,000 in 2013. Worse, the same purchasing power will cost over $200,000 in 2038. This has a huge impact on how much you need to save for your future retirement.

STEP 4. *Run the Monte Carlo Simulation on the Model*

No, it doesn't mean traveling to the Riviera

Though the model discussed above is helpful, it is also slightly inaccurate, so this extra step is intended to help fix that flaw. We all know that inflation rates will change over time and that projected rates of return will not be consistent each year, given the volatility of markets and unpredictable changes in macroeconomic business cycles. The probability of variations in these factors must also be inserted into the computer modeling to add a dose of reality to the results.

To do this, professionals often use what is called a **Monte Carlo simulation,** which has nothing to do with casinos. A Monte Carlo simulation is a sophisticated mathematical exercise that performs the calculations 10,000 different times using various ranges of inflation and rates of returns. By testing many different scenarios using the model's data, one can account for the uncertainty and inconsistency of the real world. The final product of a Monte Carlo simulation yields a percentage that represents the odds of the portfolio meeting the investor's long-term goals.

A Monte Carlo result of 100% suggests that, given all of the possible variations of inflation and RORs, there is a high chance the portfolio will meet its objectives. Of course, it is nearly impossible to get a result of 100%. Any percentage below that indicates the ROR may possibly be insufficient to reach the goal.

Let's say an investor has selected an ROR of 5%, but the Monte Carlo simulation delivers a result of 40%. This means that there is only a 4 in 10 chance that the portfolio will produce enough returns to last the person's lifetime and leave a residual amount for heirs or charitable bequeathal.

The rule of thumb I use is that Monte Carlo results of less than 70% require you to make adjustments to one of the following variables:

- **Lifestyle.** You must lower your estimated cost of living so that your cash flows can match your monthly or annual expenses.

- **Asset base.** You must increase your asset base to generate higher returns from your principal.

- **Risk tolerance.** You must be willing to take on a greater risk to achieve a higher ROR.

Making any of these three modifications in your wealth management strategy means going back to the drawing board and rethinking some of the fundamental elements of your planning. If the Monte Carlo simulation proves that you are unlikely to have enough money for your lifestyle over the remaining decades of your life, something has to change.

In general, I like to explore novel ways that people can reduce their monthly expenses without significantly altering their lifestyle or comfort. I might evaluate their priorities in terms of the residual amounts they want to leave heirs or charitable organizations. I might investigate if they have other capital assets, such as real estate or artwork, that could be sold now to increase their principal investment, enabling it to generate higher returns. Finally, I might examine the investor's risk profile and discuss whether they can or should accept higher risks. Changing someone's risk profile, however, is the last and least preferred adjustment I would recommend in doing a financial plan, as I do not agree with encouraging investors to accept risks greater than they can tolerate or which are beyond their comfort zone.

Hedging Bets with a Monte Carlo Simulation

Computers are amazing "what if" thinkers, able to perform financial projections faster and more efficiently than the human brain. A Monte Carlo simulation runs tens of thousands of scenarios, taking into account many variables all at once—rate of return, inflation, taxes, and others. The simulation generates a graphic that looks like this.

From this analysis, one can derive the highest probability that the ROR and risk level selected will achieve the desired goals. In essence, the Monte Carlo simulation helps investors see if they are being too aggressive by taking on too much risk to achieve the financial returns they need.

In some cases, I recommend to people that their goals require risk that they should not accept, should the worst case scenario for all the variables occur. Like the captain of a ship getting ready to set sail who uses a computer to project the chances of a safe journey, you want to know the worst case scenario: Is there a high probability of a "perfect storm"—winds, high seas and enormous waves. In the same way, no investor wants to set sail if there is a perfect storm on the horizon.

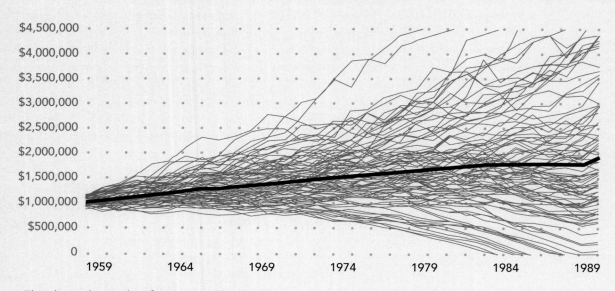

This shows the results of a Monte Carlo simulation, which runs a projected investment scenario thousands of times using different variables. The result provides a level of confidence about the probability of achieving the desired return on investment.

Next Steps?

Creating the right portfolio for wealth

Now you know your personal ROR. The next question is: How can you create the right portfolio to meet your goals over the long term? What mix of financial instruments should be selected to obtain the ROR you need? How can you avoid catastrophic loss due to unexpected market declines? How can you protect your assets from unnecessary risks? Turn the page to find out the answers.

CHAPTER FOUR

The Keys *to* SMART Asset Allocation

HOW TO CYA—COVER YOUR ASSETS— TO PROTECT FROM LOSSES

> " Always keep your investment portfolio and your risk at your own individual comfortable sleeping point. "
> —*Mario Gabelli*

ONCE YOU KNOW YOUR ROR, YOU can establish an investment strategy to achieve your goal. This is where my own advice and philosophy of investing differs from many wealth management companies and investment firms.

As I said before, I believe the stock market is the best investment vehicle to grow wealth. Based on my extensive and ongoing study of market history and research into individual company performance, as well as by following trends in the many market sectors and paying close attention to the business cycles of the US domestic economy and global economic indicators, I suggest placing the majority of an investment into the stock market.

One of the first distinguishing differences in my philosophy of investing is that I do not invest in mutual funds, index funds, or exchange traded funds (ETFs), nor do I subscribe to the "modern portfolio theory" of investing. Rather, I actively work to create a strong "asset allocation plan"—and then select the right stocks, bonds, and several other investment instruments to achieve investment goals. I then monitor the investments regularly, buying and selling stocks as needed according to many factors, such as company performance, sector trends, and various economic indicators.

In this chapter, I will first explain four strategic principles I abide by, followed by a detailed explanation of the asset allocation process that I use. Getting this step right is one of the most challenging elements of my **SMART** investment strategy. The goal is to find the right mix of assets that will deliver optimal results for building wealth. There are many financial instruments that can be used, and each plays a different role in a portfolio.

The more knowledge you have about each type of investment instrument, the **SMART**er you can be at creating an optimal portfolio.

VARIETY IS THE SPICE OF LIFE.

PRINCIPLE I:

Avoid Investment Instruments that Charge Fees

Why you don't want to buy into mutual funds or ETFs

When it comes to investing their money, many people fall into a very deep hole called 'mutual funds.' Mutual funds are groups of individual stocks or other investment instruments selected by a manager or management company that are bundled under a single name for a specific purpose. The results of the fund are thus based on the overall performance of the group collectively. Mutual funds are priced at the end of each day, reflecting the collective results of the group on that day.

Since the proliferation of mutual funds beginning in the 1960s, people have been drawn to them believing that they are the best place to invest their money for the future. The rationale for this is that mutual funds offer investors the appearance of diversification. With tens of thousands of funds to choose from, investors feel they can select from a wide variety of funds representing different investment goals and/or different industries and thus protect themselves. Some of the most common types of mutual funds include:

- **Growth (aka, capital appreciation) mutual funds:** which select stocks that will increase in value and thus be worth more in the future.

- **Balanced (aka, income & growth) mutual funds:** which select a combination of bonds for income and stocks for capital appreciation.

- **Industry sector funds:** which buy only stocks of companies in a certain industry such as energy, utilities, biotechnology, banking, and so on.

- **Retirement year directed mutual funds:** which invest in a regularly changing mix of stocks as the years go by and approach the date in the fund's name (e.g., Freedom 2020). This is because the fund seeks to invest more

conservatively as it moves towards the retirement year.

- **Bond mutual funds:** which invest in specific types of bonds reflecting the investment goal of the fund, such as municipal bonds, corporate bonds, junk bonds, and so on.

These are just some of the many categories of mutual funds. The field has expanded rapidly in the last few decades. Investors often believe they reduce their risk by investing in mutual funds. Because the fund itself contains so many different stocks or bonds, the rationale is that the poor performance of one or several companies will be counterbalanced by the better performance of others in the fund. This 'micro-diversification' is often enhanced when investors spread their money over many different types of mutual funds, rationalizing that further diversification is even better protection against loss.

However, there are problems with an investment strategy that utilizes mutual funds for the bulk of the investment. First, most mutual funds charge operating fees for the privilege of being managed. Called 12b1 fees or expense ratios, these can range anywhere from ½ percent to 5 percent per year upfront for 12b1 fees, and sometimes more, of the amount invested. Expense ratios are charged annually. It doesn't matter whether the fund makes money or loses money—the fee is still deducted from the investor's account each year. When mutual funds quote their average 1-year, 3-year, 5-year, and/or 10-year returns, the number usually includes the cost of those fees.

Furthermore, if you hire a wealth management company, or subscribe to a wealth management program at a bank or brokerage house that charges you a management fee, paying mutual fund fees becomes even more costly. Effectively, you are paying a manager to choose or recommend mutual funds that also charge you a fee. It's fees upon fees.

For many investors, tax efficiency is an important factor when investing. Unfortunately, most mutual funds are not tax efficient.

Since fund managers are investing one large pool of investments for thousands of investors, they cannot consider one individual's tax circumstances.

The most significant problem with mutual funds as your primary investment vehicle is that they are just as subject to dramatic market swings. Putting a large amount of one's wealth into a few funds, believing you are diversifying and thus mitigating the risk, does not eliminate the fact that mutual funds can get hit by a dramatic drop in the market. If you recall 2008, millions of investors in mutual funds lost as much as 40 to 50 percent of their wealth when the market tanked. In addition, mutual funds, unlike stocks, do not allow the use of risk management tools such as stop loss orders (which we will cover shortly).

For these reasons, I do not utilize mutual funds as a vehicle to grow wealth. Instead, following an active asset allocation management program can achieve far better results than mutual funds over both the short and long term.

How Global Are the World Financial Markets?

Decades ago, global economies were not correlated. A recession in Europe was unlikely to affect the economic cycle in the US or other parts of the world. This led to investment philosophies such as Modern Portfolio Theory. This theory and others like it espoused that since global economic cycles were uncorrelated, investors should diversify across all parts of the world to smooth out differences in economic and stock market cycles in the US, thus providing a more consistent rate of return with less risk.

These theories, though still popular, have become particularly inaccurate in the past 15 years, mostly because the premise on which they were based is no longer valid. Global economies have become significantly interrelated in the past two decades. Trade is no longer measured domestically, but internationally. What happens in China affects the US and the rest of the globe and vice versa.

We now live in a world where the economic cycle is global in nature and is correlated! A theory of broad global diversification to reduce risk just doesn't work! Great examples of this change in financial markets can be seen in the bear market of 2008. During this period of catastrophic market loss, all economies declined rapidly at once—and stock prices declined precipitously with them. Remember this . . . it's a global economic cycle.

Don't Invest in Index Funds

You're still risking the potential for catastrophic losses

Many brokerage houses offer investors the option to purchase index funds. Index funds are groups of stocks that are compiled together to track and match the performance of common stock market indexes, such as the S&P 500, the Dow, the Russell 2000, and others. In other words, index funds do not try to "beat the market" but simply perform exactly as the market does, given that historically, the stock market has always produced the best returns. If the S&P rises 6 percent in one year, index funds that mimic the S&P will have as their benchmark to perform nearly the same. On the other hand, if the S&P falls 3 percent in a given year, the fund's choice of stocks will very likely experience a similar loss.

Given that their goal is to match the market, this strategy needs very little day-to-day operational management. Many investors have moved to index funds because their fees are minimal, sometimes as low as 1/10 of 1%.

The problem with index funds is that, like mutual funds, they are subject to the market's ups and downs. A dramatic short-term nosedive brings on the specter of the "ugly math" I discussed, when investors may lose 10 or 20 percent of their principal but the market needs to rise 12 or 25 percent just to get back to the original amount.

For this reason, and the fact that index funds do not allow for the use of stop loss orders, do not invest in index funds. Low fees or not, I know that my active asset allocation program is far superior in achieving higher returns, with less risk, over both the short term and long term.

PRINCIPLE 3:

Don't Follow Modern Portfolio Theory

The buy and hold strategy no longer works

In the 1970s, several financial experts studied the markets and developed what came to be known as the "modern portfolio theory" as the best way to invest. They researched historical records of market returns from around the globe, and recognized that markets followed identifiable patterns. When certain types of investments such as stocks rose, bonds tended to decline. When US domestic stocks jumped, stocks in other countries crashed. When certain industrial sectors rose, others went down.

They therefore recommended that investors purchase a diversified portfolio of global stocks and bonds that would balance out these opposing market forces. Depending on the investor's age, they might recommend a portfolio of 40 percent invested in US large capitalization stocks (aka "large cap stocks"), 20 percent in US small capitalization stocks (aka, "small cap stocks"), 20 percent in foreign stocks, 10 percent in bonds, and 10 percent in cash.

According to their theory, all the investor or portfolio manager had to do was sit tight through thick and thin. Given that historically, markets always rise over the long term, the theory dictated that there was no need to buy and sell whenever one segment of the market did poorly while another did well. Things would balance out and rise eventually. The theory effectively endorsed a "buy and hold" strategy of investing. Not surprisingly, the creators of modern portfolio theory won a Nobel Prize for their research and recommendations about investing in the financial markets.

In the 1970s, 1980s, and early 1990s, investors who followed modern portfolio theory did generally well. If you diversified in the ways the theory recommended, you could achieve reasonable results. You might still encounter some periods when your investments lost value because of temporary bumps in the markets, but overall, as the theory predicted, your total returns evened out over time.

Then came the financial crash of 2008 and in one fell swoop, the theory was disproven. The reasons for this are now clear. At the end of the last century, the global financial markets were not integrated or correlated. What happened in one country did not influence others. However, this new millennium has brought vast changes. Capital markets around the world are now highly integrated. The burst of the

housing bubble in 2008 impacted nearly every developed nation as well as many emerging ones. Investors lost huge amounts of money because nearly every investment crashed at the same time—large cap, small cap, foreign stocks, and bonds.

I no longer follow modern portfolio's theory of diversification and investing. I believe that given how linked today's markets are, the theory that markets will balance is no longer accurate. Diversification according to the theory does not yield better performance nor mitigate risk. Modern portfolio's strategy of trying to diversify away risk and "buy and hold" is a "lazy man's" approach to wealth management. It's simply not rational in today's volatile, chaotic, fast-paced markets to "set it and forget it" when it comes to your investments.

PRINCIPLE 4:

Create a Customized Portfolio of Mixed Asset Classes

This is how you align with your ROR

This last principle is the crux of my philosophy of investing—each investor must formulate a customized portfolio using a mix of asset classes, calculated to deliver the ROR needed.

More importantly, each portfolio must be proactively managed to take advantage of upward market swings while minimizing the risk of drastic losses when the market declines. Portfolio management should be based on research, studying the economic cycles that influence the stock market, proactive buying and selling using fundamental analysis of companies and their profitability, and various stock market tools that help investors mitigate risk. Many of the next chapters of the book will explain these concepts in detail, so let's dig in now on the basics of asset allocation.

The Basics of Asset Allocation

What sets my philosophy apart

The active asset allocation program is a form of diversification that I recommend. It is conceived with a completely different context than modern portfolio theory. I agree that investing in a variety of stocks, bonds, and other alternatives is critical to mitigating risk, because there is still some degree of seesaw action that happens among the many types of investments. Bond returns do often decline when returns on the stock market go up, and vice versa.

However, my philosophy of asset allocation is distinctive in that it is based on selecting investments that will provide investors with the performance they need as calculated by their ROR, rather than based on balancing one's portfolio to compensate for the swings of different investment vehicles. The investor's ROR determines his or her maximum exposure to the stock market, where the risks are greatest because of market volatility.

I thus recommend that you build a portfolio with a blend of assets including:

- domestic stocks (companies based in the US),
- international stocks (stocks from global markets),
- corporate bonds,
- government bonds,
- real estate investment trusts (REITs),
- and other assets.

US and foreign stocks from the developed world play the lead role, bolstered to some degree by companies from the developing world. This is because seasoned companies tend to have the highest performance and developed stock markets tend to be the most stable.

In addition, I almost always infuse a portfolio with a percentage of fixed income assets, which can include corporate and government bonds. While these alternative assets provide lower returns than stocks, they generally have less volatility.

PRINCIPLE 8

MATCH YOUR STOCK MARKET EXPOSURE TO YOUR ROR

The SMART way to mitigate risk and create a balanced portfolio is to select a mix of assets that, when combined, works to achieve your long-term ROR. Working backwards from your ROR, you can calculate what maximum exposure you need in the stock market by weighing in the average returns of the various asset classes to determine the upper limit of stock market exposure you require.

Using Historical Performance to Calculate Your Asset Allocation

Replacing "subjective" opinion with facts

The question is, how do you determine your asset allocation so that it matches your ROR? The answer: use real historical data about assets as the basis for determining your stock exposure. Using actual facts takes the guesswork out of calculating your stock exposure, and eliminates relying on emotional or "intuitive" feelings about stocks.

You begin by looking up the historical returns of every asset class of investment, which we did back in chapter 1 (refer to page 15). Next, given these historical returns, you can perform an easy mathematical equation to calculate your asset allocation model.

Let's take an investor whose ROR calculation dictates a 10% return per year to sustain the lifestyle to which they are accustomed. Based on this historical data, the only way to reach a 10% return would be to invest all one's assets solely in the stock market. This is the only asset class that comes close to having a 10% annual return.

Of course many, if not most investors would balk at investing all their money in the stock market. It's too risky. This is one reason why I recommend that when investors prepare their ROR, they do not reach for the sky and dream of receiving a 10% or greater annual return.

To be realistic, let's take a hypothetical investor, Dr. Thomas, who seeks a more reasonable 6% ROR for his $1 million in investments. What asset allocation would achieve this? Given this modest rate of return, we know he does not require a portfolio invested solely in equities (stocks), as that would be a far higher risk level than he needs to take. Instead, he can afford to have a mixture of less volatile investments.

Dr. Thomas' portfolio can be calculated using the historical returns of assets as the chart shows to determine what combination of equities and bonds would deliver at least a 6% average annual return.

Investment $1,000,000

50% invested in stocks	40% invested in bonds
@10% return per year	@4% return per year
=$50,000 annual ROR	=$16,000 annual ROR

TOTAL $66,000 annual ROR = 6.6%

As the calculation shows, this mix of stocks and bonds (which actually only amounts to 90% of his investment, leaving 10% to be invested in other asset classes) is adequate to provide the necessary long-term ROR while mitigating Dr. Thomas' risk. If the stock market suddenly collapsed, only half of his portfolio would be affected, providing at least some degree of protection for the rest of his capital.

Of course, the calculation above is based on the assumption that the average annual returns of all asset classes will continue "as usual" going forward. As any financial advisor or wealth management firm will attest, historical returns cannot be guaranteed to predict the future. Nevertheless, the reliability of using historical returns that cover an extensive period of time, such as 30 years, is that they reflect many market cycles. Unless the market does a nosedive as severe as that of the Great Depression, the historical returns for 30 years will mimic most of the usual peaks and troughs of regular market cycles and average out to that 10% figure.

Asset Allocation Does Not Mean "Set It and Forget It"

Constant vigilance and rebalancing are necessary on a regular basis

I call this "active asset allocation" because, unlike modern portfolio theory, I do not subscribe to the assumption that once the choice of assets classes is made and specific stocks/bonds are selected, the investor's portfolio will self-correct without any interference. No matter how well diversified one's portfolio is, today's world is too unpredictable and volatile to risk any portion of one's wealth. I see no reason why investors should stand idly by and watch any portion of their investment lose significant value, based on the assumption that "things will rebalance" soon enough.

I have encountered several "retired" investors (meaning people who have enough money not to work) who thought they "had it made" in 2007. They had enough assets to meet their monthly budgets and their wealth was enough to last their lifetime at a reasonable ROR. What they did not realize was that they had far too much stock exposure relative to what they needed for their lifestyle. Then 2008 hit . . . They lost nearly 50% of their wealth, because they lacked proper risk mitigation tools to counteract their exposure in the stock market.

It took these individuals more than six years of recovery time to return to their former asset levels—and what a shame! Compounding the loss was that they had to continue withdrawing

---

PRINCIPLE 9

ALLOCATE ACCORDING TO MARKET CONDITIONS IN THE CONTEXT OF YOUR ROR

In periods of healthy global conditions, an investor's stock allocation should be at the top of their ROR range. In times of poor global conditions, an investor's stock allocation should be at the lowest end of their ROR range, or even below it if the stock market is clearly in a full decline. The principle is to "make hay while the sun shines," and "head for shelter" to protect one's assets when a storm is brewing on the horizon. This is the SMART strategy—the key to building long-term wealth.

principal and further increasing the need to have even higher long-term ROR to make their money grow back enough to last their lifetime.

You must strategically and proactively manage your portfolio of assets. You must keep adjusting your asset allocation to account for market performance, taking advantage of research and tools that can help you better see which stocks may rise and which may fall. Because the stock market goes through cycles, it is a **SMART** strategy to be vigilant and adjust your asset allocation to match the immediate time. I know that today's markets are anything but consistent. Therefore, the prudent investor must take the ideal allocation and create a range of possible options dependent on the conditions of the global business cycle.

For example, in the case of our hypothetical Dr. Thomas, we saw that a 50% stock allocation is sufficient to achieve his ROR. However, in periods of global economic turmoil and poor market conditions, he will need to own less stock to avoid the risk of catastrophic loss. Should the markets face worsening global economic conditions, Dr. Thomas would want to adjust his stock exposure down to 40%, then 30%, and even 20% or 10% if a deep recession occurs.

As a corollary to the above advice, the opposite is equally true. Investors might adjust their exposure to the stock market slightly upwards when the economy is in a boom period, but I suggest that you do not overreach. Remember, the urge to increase your stock investments is probably coming from a false sense of optimism and the emotion of greed. Don't fall into the trap that today's rising market means you should go for a stock market exposure higher than you calculated as safe.

This may seem too conservative for aggressive investors, but it is a fundamental **SMART** asset allocation rule. I strictly adhere to it. Markets are very hard to predict and even in the face of increasing optimism, they can collapse quickly (as they did in the beginning of 2016). Your asset allocation and degree of stock exposure is your first line of defense to mitigate catastrophic loss and the ugly math of recovering your assets. The lesson is to make sure that you know what your maximum stock exposure is—40%? 50%? 80%?—and watch it closely.

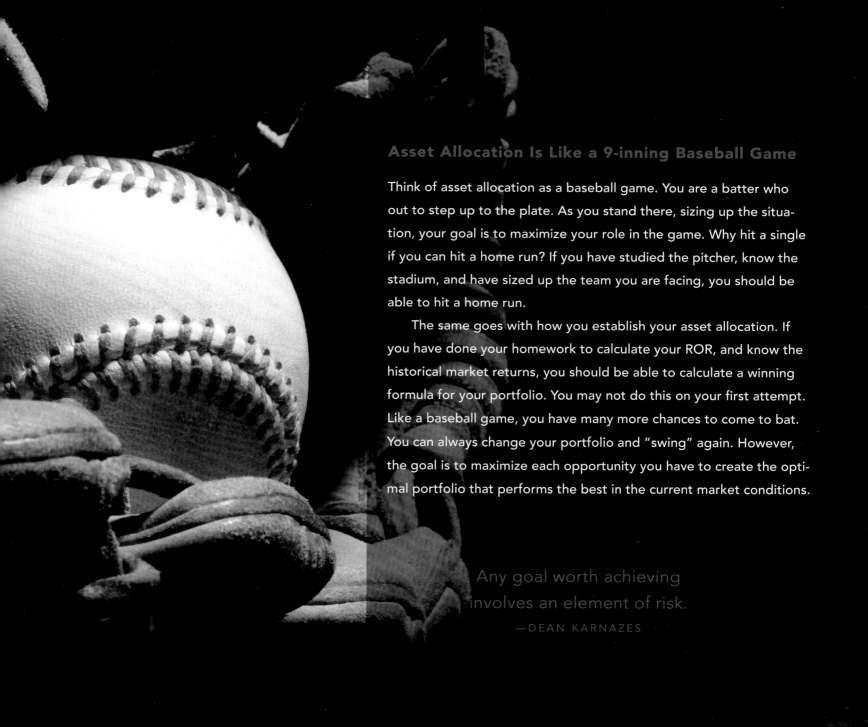

Asset Allocation Is Like a 9-inning Baseball Game

Think of asset allocation as a baseball game. You are a batter who out to step up to the plate. As you stand there, sizing up the situation, your goal is to maximize your role in the game. Why hit a single if you can hit a home run? If you have studied the pitcher, know the stadium, and have sized up the team you are facing, you should be able to hit a home run.

The same goes with how you establish your asset allocation. If you have done your homework to calculate your ROR, and know the historical market returns, you should be able to calculate a winning formula for your portfolio. You may not do this on your first attempt. Like a baseball game, you have many more chances to come to bat. You can always change your portfolio and "swing" again. However, the goal is to maximize each opportunity you have to create the optimal portfolio that performs the best in the current market conditions.

Any goal worth achieving involves an element of risk.
—DEAN KARNAZES

CHAPTER FIVE

Stay Ahead *of the* Stock Market Curve

HOW TO RIDE THE BULL AND AVOID THE BEAR

" The intelligent investor is likely to need considerable willpower to keep from following the crowd.

—*Benjamin Graham* "

IN THE LAST CHAPTERS, YOU SAW HOW establishing your own ROR and asset allocation are the driving forces behind my philosophy of investing. You also know from Chapter 2 that global stock markets run in cycles—years of rising stock prices (bull markets) and shorter periods of rapidly declining markets (bear markets).

Bull and bear markets are regular cycles of the financial markets. While they may appear to be unpredictable, there are clear signs that signal when a bull or bear market is about to happen. By recognizing these signs, you can take action to alter your asset allocation before other investors begin buying or selling stocks. Like driving a car, you can assess the traffic in advance, knowing when to put your foot on the gas versus when to reach for the brakes.

The challenges investors need to address are how to identify a bull market, understand how long it will last and what makes it special compared to those in the past. Even more important for investors is the ability to detect the signs of an oncoming bear market to avoid catastrophic loss, ugly math (described earlier), and the devastation it can cause to a well-thought-out, long-term financial plan. In this chapter, we'll identify what drives both bull and bear markets and discuss how investors can prepare and anticipate these important changes in global financial markets.

You get recessions, you have stock market declines.

If you don't understand that's going to happen,

then you're not ready; you won't do well in the markets.

—PETER LYNCH, FORMER MANAGER OF MAGELLAN FUND, FIDELITY INVESTMENTS

How Stock Market Investors Stay "Ahead of the Curve"

Understanding the business cycle is key

Most investors think that bull and bear markets are random—they are not. They are very closely linked to changes in economic conditions—what I call the "business cycle." In periods of economic growth, stock prices show a clear upward bias, whereas during economic difficulty, stock prices decline—and sometimes catastrophically fall.

The chart on the next page shows how what once looked like random changes in stock prices are highly correlated to economic conditions. The graph shows the movement of stock prices over the time period, while the vertical bars describe the economic phases during this time frame. This is a picture of the business cycles—periods of economic growth versus periods of economic weakness. The vertical gold bars indicate periods when the economy was weak or recessionary. The periods in between indicate years of economic expansion. It is clear from this chart that to be a successful investor, one needs to understand the business cycles.

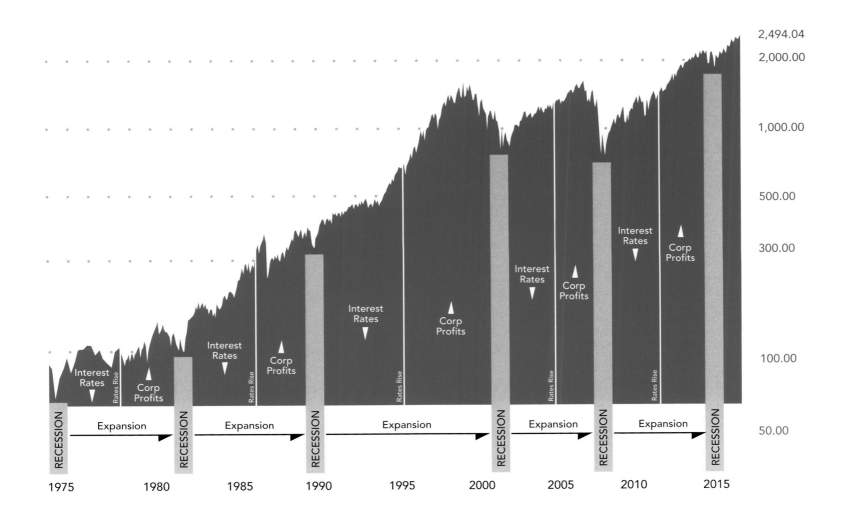

Bull and bear markets are not random. They go in cycles, linked to economic conditions.
When the economy is in expansion mode, the market tends to rise as interest rates go down and corporate profits rise.
But as the economy heats up and interest rates rise, it leads to a period of recession. This cycle repeats, on average, every 7 to 9 years.

Become a Student of Business Cycles
They tell you when and where to invest

The first step to becoming a **SMART** investor is to become a student of the business cycles. While this may sound tedious, it is actually easier and more interesting than you would think. By keeping an eye on the business cycles, you can often predict where the stock market is going.

What drives an economic and thus the stock market cycle? Which factors seem to cause stock market booms and busts? Understanding these factors is the key to identifying in advance when the stock market will climb, or when it will descend. As you will see, when you understand the business cycle, you can adjust your asset allocation in **SMART** ways to enhance your investment performance.

You will also learn what kinds or groups of stocks will likely perform best . . . and which to avoid using the business cycles as your guide. This is crucial to your Asset Allocation "Action" Plan. If you can anticipate the business cycle, you can adjust your asset allocation and groups of stocks to maximize your returns, while also mitigating risk. Various indicators often signal that an upward or downward cycle is approaching. Let's dig in!

Business Cycles Are Like Gravity—Undeniable!

It's time to learn Economics 101

Global economies do not grow at the same pace at all times. Economies fluctuate between periods of strong and weak growth, creating the business cycles. Fluctuations in the rate of economic growth are largely dependent on the relationship between the supply and demand for goods and services, which dictate the level of economic activity in a society.

Increased economic activity causes a rise in the demand and prices for goods and services. But if goods and services become too expensive, demand falls and economic activity slows. This, in turn, causes goods and services to become "cheap" again, which leads to a new cycle.

Economists often divide a business cycle into five stages:

- **Expansion:** the upward curve on a graph

- **Peak:** the top of the curve

- **Contraction:** the point at which the curve begins a downward slope

- **Trough:** the bottom of the downward slope

- **Recovery:** the point at which the curve begins a new upward slope

The Five Stages of the Business Cycle

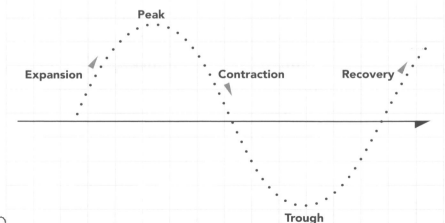

Gross Domestic Product: The Measure of Economic Growth

It's also the most significant indicator of business cycles!

GDP, which stands for Gross Domestic Product, is one of the most significant indicators of a nation's economic health. The statistic is the measure of the "value added" to all goods and services in a nation, less the value of the goods and services used up in production. In other words, it is essentially a number that reflects the total dollar value of all goods and services produced during a given period of time. Think of it as a speedometer. Higher GDP growth means the economy is growing faster... slower GDP means the economy is slowing down or growing slowly. An economy that is not growing will have a GDP of zero.

Building a car provides a good example for understanding what numbers are used to calculate GDP. GDP doesn't effectively measure the cost of the steel itself, but rather the "value added" by the car manufacturer to produce the car.

If the steel had been added into GDP, it would have been double counted.

GDP is effectively used to track a nation's economic production. By measuring GDP quarter over quarter, it is possible to see if a nation's economy (or even the whole global economy) is growing or shrinking.

In the US, the ideal GDP growth rate is considered to be between 2% and 4% annually. If the GDP is lower, the economy risks a slowdown or recession. If the GDP is higher, it may mean the economy is overheating, with investors pouring money into speculative ventures.

An annualized GDP higher than 5% might be moving towards an inflationary period, which in turn can lead to economic and stock market bubbles that are very dangerous for investors. As you will learn later, GDP is one of the key indicators to watch when you are investing in stocks, not just for making your buy and sell decisions, but even what stocks to buy and sell. By understanding the economic cycle, investors can maximize their rate of return and minimize risk.

Business Cycles Are Regularly Irregular

They may vary between 6 to 9 years

At one time, business cycles were thought to be extremely regular, with predictable durations, but today they are widely acknowledged to be irregular, varying in frequency, magnitude and duration. The view is that in today's world, they persist on average between 6 and 9 years, peak to peak.

Given how complex the modern global economy has become, there is little about it that is totally predictable. Within the last decade, China, Brazil, and India have become significant players in the global economy, influencing the ups and downs of business in the US. Each of these economies has their own central bank policies and idiosyncrasies, of which investors need to be aware. Let's face it, if business cycles were highly predictable, investing would be very easy!

Here are some key facts about business cycles that can help investors understand when to buy or sell:

- According to the National Bureau of Economic Research (NBER), there have been a total of 34 business cycles in the US since 1854. From 1854 to 1919, there were 16 cycles, with the average recession lasting

22 months. Since 1945, economic expansions have been longer lasting, 57 months, while recessions are getting shorter, just 12 months on average. This might reflect the improved capabilities of economists and government central banks to control the economic cycles when they become perturbed.

- For the past 30 years in particular, economic expansions have tended to be longer in duration than recessions. The average duration of an expansion over the past 30 years has been 6–9 years versus the average duration of a recession at only 11 months. During this 30-year period, no expansions have lasted less than 5 years. Conclusion: Expansions seem to last longer than recessions. Therefore, if we are in an expansion, it can be a good long run for profit-making in the stock market. In fact, over the past 45 years the average stock market advance during an expansion has been a whopping 150% to over 300%!

- During the same time frame, recessions, though shorter, have been particularly brutal. The average decline of stock prices during a recession has been 39.87%! Even worse, the last two recessions have seen stock markets fall by more than 50%!

These facts bring to light the importance of riding the bull and avoiding the bear for maximum wealth creation.

There are exceptions even to the irregular nature of business cycles. The Great Depression, which saw its most substantial decline in economic activity from 1929 to 1933, lasted more than three years (43 months to be exact), and then it was still followed by seven more years of very slow growth until WWII began. The 2008 Great Recession took seven years to recover from. The lesson is that some business cycles will surprise us, requiring patience and a **SMART** investment strategy.

Why Do Expansions Have Longer Life Cycles Compared to Recessions?

Here is my take on it. I suggest it has to do with the fact that during recessions, all of the excess production and consumer and corporate spending that had been generated during the expansion is wrung out of the system. As soon as companies predict a recessionary period coming, they stop producing at the same pace, and allow excess inventories to get used up. This decreases their spending little by little.

At some point down the road in this retraction, nothing is left, leaving very little room for further downside. Indeed, if the recession is a "normal" one, then at some point, all inventories get used up and companies must begin producing again. This actually helps raise the economy slowly back up towards an expansion. If the government gives the economic system some kind of stimulus (see sidebar on The Role of Central Banks), it adds greater impetus to a rebound. It can take years to wind the economy back up to full speed, making expansions seem to last for years.

Terms Used to Talk about Business Cycles

Go to the head of the class by knowing these terms!

ECONOMIC EXPANSION:
The best environment for all stocks!

In an economic expansion, GDP growth is at an annualized rate of 2% to 3% and possibly rising. As a result, consumers feel confident about spending, and their purchasing habits drive businesses to increase production and hire more workers. Many workers also receive salary increases and/or bonuses, giving them more disposable income to spend. An economic expansion can feed upon itself, creating a cycle of increasing prosperity, production, and profits.

ECONOMIC RECESSION:
The worst environment for most stocks

A recession occurs when a business cycle moves in a downward trend and creates a significant contraction period of much lower demand for goods and services than normal. Recessions are defined as a period of significant decline in economic activity (as reflected in the GDP) that lasts at least two or more consecutive quarters (3 months) of time.

Recessions can trigger periods of deflation. As people stop purchasing goods and services, there is greatly reduced economic activity, which also puts pressure on jobs. As opportunities for work plummet, there is increasing potential for people to be laid off, creating a cycle of higher unemployment.

In the US, the National Bureau of Economic Research (NBER) is the government agency that tracks economic activity and business cycles, and makes an official pronouncement if the US has entered into a recession. Unfortunately, NBER data is of little use. Historically, by the time government statisticians have figured out that the economy is in a recession, it's way too late and a recovery may be close at hand. Therefore, **SMART** investors must use their own process and analysis to anticipate recessions and the ensuing recoveries.

ECONOMIC DEPRESSION: The worst environment for nearly all stocks and people!

A depression is essentially a lengthy and severe recession that goes on for years and causes substantially lower production of goods and services, lackluster consumer purchases, high levels of unemployment, reduced trade, many company and personal bankruptcies, and a pullback in offering credit to businesses and individuals. Economists differ in how to precisely define a depression, but the general rule is that it is a period marked by either of two factors:

1 A decline in real GDP greater than 10%, or

2 A recession lasting 2 or more years.

Some economists demarcate a depression as the period starting from the peak of a business cycle downward until the trough bottoms out and begins to rise. Other economists say a depression begins at the peak of an economic

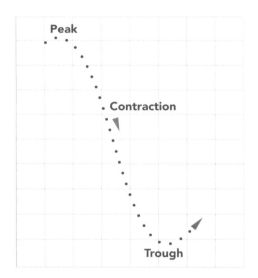

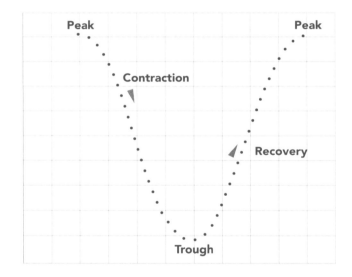

Different economists define a depression differently. Some say it starts when the peak of an expansion declines and lasts through the moment the trough turns upward (left graphic). Others say it lasts from one peak till the next peak (right graphic).

cycle and lasts until the economy has returned to that same peak.

Whichever definition is used, a depression always has the same starting point as a recession. A recession evolves into a depression by persisting for years.

Historically, the term has been reserved only for the period that began in 1929 and lasted until 1939, which has come to be known as The Great Depression. Even the economic downturn that started in 2007 and lasted through 2009 is called The Great Recession. Economists probably fear using the word "depression" again, lest history repeats itself.

INFLATION:
Not good for stocks or people

In a free market, prices can rise and fall based on supply and demand. During "normal" times, some prices might rise slightly each year, while others fall. However, there are times when the market experiences a lot of price increases, causing inflation. This can happen when the business cycle is in a steep upward climb and many prices are rising simultaneously. This can cause an "abnormal" blip in pricing, when prices go higher than what is considered normal.

Although it would seem to be a positive market force to have an upward business cycle, if it results in a period of severe inflation, the purchasing power of money decreases. In an inflationary period, what cost $1.00 last year costs $1.04 this year at a 4% inflation rate. This may seem small in the context of $1.00, but when multiplied out, it can amount to a great deal. A 4% inflation rate on an annual budget of $50,000 means you'd need to have an extra $2,000 to purchase the same amount of goods and services.

Long periods of inflation can ultimately disrupt the business cycle and significantly slow it down. Inflation lowers economic production, and tends to create anxiety for investors who become concerned that their investments will not keep up with the declining purchasing power of their money. This investor anxiety can affect the forward movement of financial markets.

The Role of Government Central Banks to Smooth out Markets

Ever since modern economics was founded, experts have been trying to better understand the causes of business and stock market cycles and to learn ways to control them more tightly. Today's economists have made progress in this regard. The global financial markets are much more stable today than they were when the Great Depression hit in the 1930s. Our ability to keep the 2008 financial crisis at the level of a Great Recession rather than a second Great Depression is a bittersweet testament to the knowledge that economists have been able to learn from history about how to keep the world from the brink of a total financial collapse.

One of the chief tools in the economists' toolbox is a government-run central bank that performs various functions to regulate the financial markets in a country. The concept of a "central bank" originated as far back as 1694 when the Bank of England was formed to loan money to the English government. It took many more decades for the notion of a central bank as an economic stabilizer to catch on in other European countries.

Central banks were created to regulate the value of a nation's currency, print its bank notes, and be "the lender of last resort" to banks throughout that country when economic crises loomed and threatened to curtail the flow of money, especially loans to the growing businesses of the mercantile era.

Today, most of the world's governments maintain a central bank that is responsible for monitoring the country's economic activity and tracking the indicators of inflation, recession, and depression. In modern economic theory, effective central bank policy is the equivalent of wise interference to keep the economy from going too deep into either recession or into an inflationary period. By taking certain actions during economic slumps, such as reducing the "federal funds interest rate" so that businesses can still borrow money for investing and paying their employees, the central bank provides the necessary economic stimulus that can reduce the severity of a downturn. In times of inflation, the central bank can raise interest rates, slowing down growth to rein in increasing prices.

Central banks must make decisions with great caution. If they do nothing to alter interest rates when the economy is climbing or descending too fast, they could provoke an inflationary period or a recession. If they adjust interest rates too high, it could exacerbate an ongoing inflationary period by leading to stagnation when the economy stalls. If they lower interest rates too far, they could trigger borrowing excesses that lead investors to bid up the expected future value of stocks and bonds to dangerously high levels.

DEFLATION:
Also not good for stocks or people

Deflation, the opposite of inflation, is when the inflation rate falls to very low levels or below 0%. Deflation is effectively the result of a substantially lower demand for goods and services, which causes prices to fall. For example, in a deflationary period, what cost you $1.00 last year may only cost you 98 cents, a deflation rate of 2%. This may sound great, but in a period of deflation, falling prices may cause consumers and businesses to delay new purchases and consumption, thinking that goods and services will be cheaper if they just wait. In turn this can lead to businesses lowering prices in an attempt to motivate buyer demand again. It soon becomes a downward spiraling cycle, disrupting the normal economic pattern in which prices slowly rise over time as costs of supplies and labor increase.

Deflation can be a problem for investors because lower prices drive interest rates and stock market returns down for certain sectors. Banks cannot loan to businesses at less than 0% and governments cannot pay high interest rates on bonds to stimulate the economy when there is deflation. As a result, investors often hoard their money, not wanting to take increased risks for their returns. This, too, reduces economic output and creates investor anxiety.

PRINCIPLE 10

BUSINESS FUNDAMENTALS ARE MORE IMPORTANT THAN EMOTIONS

The basic rule of thumb in investing is that the long-term view of the underlying fundamentals of a business cycle will always prevail in determining the pricing valuations of most financial instruments. This is why many financial analysts and investors operate according to the theory that markets are 'efficient,' meaning that the investment values are based not on fleeting emotions or temporary trends, but on real facts about assets and their long-term value.

The Strong Link between Business Cycles and the Value of Assets

SMART investors stay ahead of the economic cycle

Whatever stage of the business cycle is occurring in a particular country has the greatest influence on the behavior of all investment markets in that country—stocks, bonds, real estate, gold, silver and so on. As I mentioned previously, national business cycles are increasingly affected by events internationally. In effect, it is fair to say that over the intermediate- and long-term horizon, the price of just about every financial instrument mirrors the behavior of the underlying economic backdrop of the world. Research has shown that the business cycle and each of its stages are responsible for nearly 100% of the fluctuation of asset prices such as stocks, bonds, and real estate over the long term.

What's interesting about this connection is the fact that investors behave in a way that actually precedes the business cycle. This is because savvy investors bid stocks higher or lower based on their knowledge of economic cycles and their ability to "read between the lines" and recognize whether the economy is growing, slowing,

peaking, or receding. Investors collectively buy or sell investments to reflect their opinion of the market value of each asset class at any given time, based on how they view the underlying "economic fundamentals," meaning the basic indicators of the business cycle's health. These fundamentals include such factors as the unemployment rate, productivity, inflation, GDP rate of growth, and many other indicators that I will discuss in this book. If it appears to investors that the business cycle will go up, most financial instruments will gain value. If it seems the business cycle will soon descend, most financial instruments will equally lose value.

The chart on the next page shows the correlation of the stock market and business cycles. One can easily see that ahead of periods of expansions, stocks show an early upward bias in advance of the actual business cycle upward movement. Similarly, before the peak of an upward cycle, investors recognize when an economic decline is upcoming, and begin bidding down the price of stocks.

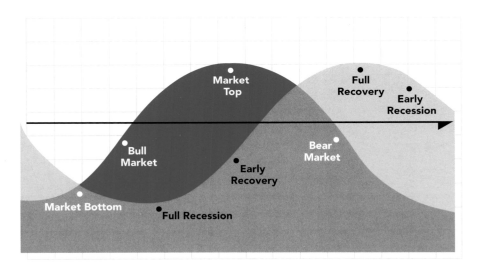

STOCK MARKET CYCLE   **BUSINESS CYCLE**

Investors can stay ahead of the curve by paying attention to the business cycle. Here, we can see that stock market changes precede the business cycle.

In this way, the stock market rise or falls ahead of the curve. **SMART** investors are savvy folks. By researching and studying companies, reading their reports and press releases, and looking for clues in the economic trends that might affect a company's sales, these investors can often make a highly educated guess about a company's future performance. Expecting profits to rise, they know that latecomer investors will be willing to pay more for a stock and therefore tend to bid its price higher than the company's actual current value. In this way, the current stock price of some companies often has built into it an already expected higher valuation reflecting future profits.

The opposite is equally true. The stock market is also efficient in discounting stock prices when savvy investors predict periods of lackluster profit growth or even periods of declining sales and profits. During recessions, corporate sales and profits tumble quickly. The stock market reflects this in advance by reducing the value of stocks even faster than the drop in profits, as investors now want to stay ahead of the downward curve.

Investor Psychology Plays a Role, Too

Fear and greed get the best of us!

There is a small percentage of stock market fluctuations that are not due to investors following the business cycle, but rather are a function of investor psychology. It is widely known that investors make poor investment decisions. They panic sell at market bottoms and overinvest at market tops. These bad decisions generate terrible results and ruined financial plans. It's our human nature—that little voice in our head—that makes us fearful or greedy—at just the wrong time.

Investor psychology thus plays a role in the status of the financial markets, though usually just in terms of short-term results. Fear, greed, anxiety, euphoria, and other sorts of investor emotions can definitely affect what happens to financial markets on an immediate basis. What is reported in the media can also play a minor role, such as provoking a short-term buying or selling frenzy.

The following graphic illustrates investor psychology about stock market cycles. It speaks volumes about how people gain confidence as they become greedy, and then lose confidence as they finally realize their mistakes.

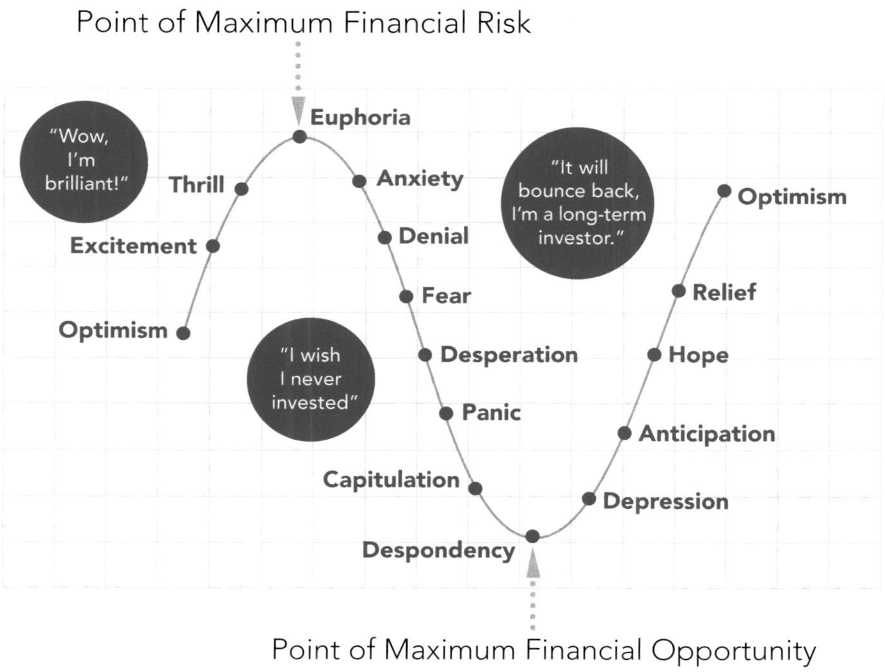

Point of Maximum Financial Risk

"Wow, I'm brilliant!"

Euphoria

Thrill

Anxiety

Excitement

Denial

Fear

Optimism

"It will bounce back, I'm a long-term investor."

Optimism

Relief

"I wish I never invested"

Desperation

Hope

Panic

Anticipation

Capitulation

Depression

Despondency

Point of Maximum Financial Opportunity

THE HUMAN BRAIN IS NOT GOOD AT INVESTING

However, research indicates that investor and "crowd" psychology often price securities based on incorrect information. In the late 1990's, for example, investors had a love affair with tech stocks, and pushed valuations far above realistic pricing. Most of these tech securities became extremely overvalued, and this created a bubble that eventually burst and caused significant losses.

If investors had been mindful that the market was not "efficiently" or correctly pricing these securities, they may have behaved differently. Moreover, at that point, the economic cycle was already in its ninth year, so the **SMART** asset allocation investor would have recognized that the market would soon decline, and taken steps to be 30% less invested!

The lesson here is: the market is usually but not always efficient. Understanding the business cycle can help you understand the difference and use it to your advantage!

So What Are the Lessons of Economic Cycles and Psychology?

Four key pieces of advice for investors

There are four critical lessons you can learn from this chapter about business cycles and investor psychology.

1 Invest as soon as signs indicate an expansion. When signs point to a growing economy, it is highly likely that most companies will experience increasing demand for their goods and services. Increased consumer confidence usually leads to greater sales, and profits thus rise across most consumer sectors and industries, such as technology products, automobiles, home appliances, industrial machinery, clothing, and food products, to name just a few. A booming economy also tends to drive up energy consumption, as businesses need more energy to run their factories and operations. Many industries feed off of each other, with the increased sales of some products and services producing a domino effect by encouraging increased sales of other products and services. The companies that make these sales have the potential to realize significant profit growth and hence are worth more as entities. This is the time to invest.

2 Don't get overly excited during expansions. When the economy is growing, the news is great on CNBC and stocks are rising every day, it is tempting to increase your stock exposure beyond its maximum allocation as determined by your ROR. Most investors let the excitement of expanding markets get the best of them and begin overinvesting. When markets go up a lot, the human brain says "I need more and more!" when in fact it should be restraining you from letting greed take over your investing.

I remember well how, in the rosy market of 2007, many investors thought they should simply keep increasing their stock allocation given the market strength. In times like this, you have to keep a level head, reminding yourself of two things: 1. sometimes risking too much is unnecessary for the success of your long-term plan; and 2. you have to keep an eye on the business cycle as a rosy market occurring at the end of an aging cycle, such as 2007, may look great right until it ends badly, as it did in 2008.

③ Don't wait too long when the signals predict a recession. When markets begin falling, there is first a tendency for people to sit tight with their stocks, believing that "things will come back," and they will quickly regain their losses. In some cases, this may be true, but if you follow the signals about the business cycle, you will be much better at recognizing when it is just wishful thinking. Sometimes it's not a light at the end of the tunnel, but an oncoming train!

Successful investing is anticipating the anticipation of others.
—JOHN MAYNARD KEYNES

In 2008, for instance, I was sad to read that many investors never sold any stock before the stock market completely tanked. We know the terrible psychology that exists for most investors when markets start to decline. That little voice says "this is only temporary; it will recover," and then the market falls further... and the little voice says "well I'm not selling now, it's way too low!" and it falls further yet again, until the investor denies that it even exists and the losses are ugly. I call these investors the "hangers on." They hang on way too long!

The most dangerous words in investing.

4 **Don't avoid the market when it bottoms.**
There is also a tendency for people who are "hangers on" to suddenly sell. Denial turns to fear and panic, and they make a mad rush to the exit . . . often selling at or close to the bottom of the market cycle. This behavior just doesn't make any sense. These investors are running out, just when they should be running in! Their low-ball selling completely ruins their long-term financial plans.

The perfect time to enter the stock market is when the economy is coming out of a recession. One reason is that recessions knock the stuffing out of the economy . . . and out of people, too. Investors often get so "spooked" during a recession that they fail to reenter the market until most of the recovery has played out. In their fear, they miss out on the biggest upside growth potential.

Surprisingly, during every economic recession and expansion, the bulk of the investing community (often referred to as "the crowd") behaves this way. It is uncanny!

This behavior is the reverse of what **SMART** investors should be doing. Immediately after a recession is precisely the time to aggressively invest in the market, selecting those companies that will outperform others in the upswing—and fill your portfolio with those. Unfortunately, many investors (and there are a lot of you according to the statistics) tend not to get back into the market until it has risen substantially years later. When it appears to be "safe" again you've missed the period of time in which you could have made enormous profits on the business cycle upswing.

Three Caveats about Stock Market Investing

One for everyone, one for baby boomers, and one for millennials

Before we leave this chapter, I want to convey three caveats about investing in the stock market.

❶ Never use recent short-term results as indicative of the future

Investors often decide how much stock exposure to have in their portfolio based on recent stock price performance. If the stock market has done well, investors have a tendency to "pile in" after the rise. They experience a false sense of confidence from rising markets and think that the upward trend will *definitely* continue forever... at least while *they* are in the market!

This myopia is somewhat understandable. It is a natural human tendency to think optimistically and to make decisions based on gut feelings about the market. A rising stock market encourages people to feel positive about the future.

They forget history, focusing only on the immediate time period. Greed—the thought of making a huge profit in the next few months or within a year—takes over rational thinking. Even **SMART** investors who know that markets crash in cycles often disregard the warning signs, believing "this time is different." It is usually not.

The higher markets rise, the more investors feel confident and the more "crowd thinking" leads people to believe they should place all their assets in stocks. After all, everyone else is doing it. As we know from history, though, this usually ends badly. Investors pour money into a rising stock market and become most fully invested just as stock markets are about to shift downwards.

Of course, the reverse psychological effect on investors is equally true in poor market conditions. If stocks have fallen recently or for a few months, there is a tendency for investors to reduce their stock holdings, believing the market will continue to tumble. The further stocks fall, the more investors sell. This too ends badly, for just as investors have lost faith in stocks and reduced most of their holdings, the markets often rebound, leaving those investors in the dust.

Although both these behaviors are common for the bulk of investors (including institutional investors), they are usually driven by emotion. This is counterproductive to optimizing long-term returns and reaching your long-term personal ROR. **SMART** investors do not allow emotion and recent global stock market performance to dictate how much of their portfolio is composed of stocks.

Instead, investors should stick to a scientific approach—one that removes the emotional bias, focusing on meaningful and factual indicators of the economic cycle as well as the fundamentals of each company in which they invest (discussed in a later chapter). Buying and selling stocks needs to be done according to well-timed orders that take advantage of market trends and specific company reports. A scientific approach puts the odds in the investor's favor to win in the marketplace.

2 You probably have a false historical perspective if you are a baby boomer

A second reason some investors miss out on bull markets is that they just don't have any grounding in history. For baby boomers, who began investing in the stock market when they were in their late 20s, 30s, and 40s, their understanding of the market is heavily based on the boom years of the 1980s and 1990s, decades when the market was rocking and rolling.

The average *annual* return for stocks as measured by the S&P 500 was a whopping 18 percent from 1982 through 1999! Though stocks experienced short-term volatility during those decades—the period included two recessions and the crash of 1987 when the S&P fell 20 percent—share prices always recovered and managed to advance to new highs. This was an era of little downward change in the market, with significant global economic growth on the opportunities brought about by tremendous advances in technology. Many new companies were born during those decades, which today number among the most successful and profitable companies in the world.

Those historical decades have given many baby boomers the mindset that today's stock market still operates the same way as those great years. Yes, there are a few declines here and there, but otherwise, the market experiences solid double-digit annual growth that goes on indefinitely. It's no wonder that boomers were unprepared for the "lost decade" of 2000–2010, and they continue to be unprepared for the rollicking stock market of this new century.

If you are a baby boomer, beware . . . today's stock market is different than it was 20 years ago. Much has changed and if you have not kept up with the changes, you are in for a surprise and a disappointment. You cannot expect the high growth the market generated in the 80s and 90s. The bull markets of those two decades may have produced tremendous wealth for some, but it also created a warped sense of reality for both individual and institutional investors.

Most boomer-generation individual investors and finance committees that were active in the late 1990's continue to believe in unrealistic future growth rates. They often base their monthly living expense budgets on past stock market returns that allowed them to retire and live like "royalty." Many disregarded investment alternatives, believing that only stocks could produce above-average returns. Meanwhile, low-yielding bonds were considered to be only for the very elderly, who cannot afford to take risks.

This mindset causes many of today's boomer investors, both institutional and individual, to invest without realistic long-term objectives, performance targets, spending policies or respect for risk. They feel driven to "beat the market," but it is now harder and harder to do so.

If you are a baby boomer, you have to scale back or "normalize" your expectations. The above-norm performance of stock indexes in your youthful years, and the unavoidable greed associated with a rising market, may have fostered in you a false sense of short-term expectations, above index performance obsession, and a complete disregard for risk. This type of groupthink will prove to be dangerous to the long-term objectives and unattended risk tolerance of our new century, especially if you are a boomer approaching retirement.

3 You probably lack historical perspective if you are a millennial

Millennials, who are defined as those born between 1985 and 2001, know little about the significant market panics that happened when they were toddlers or teenagers. Your view of the stock market has been formed largely in the last decade. For many of you, the Great Recession of 2007–2008 comprises a good portion of your stock market knowledge. You may feel uneasy about investing in stocks, or at least uncertain about whether it is a wise decision to put your money there. You may opt for managed mutual funds, believing that they are safer, without knowing that historically, their performance lags behind stocks.

You Too Can Stay Ahead of the Curve

Now you know about business cycles and their effect on the stock market. You have a good understanding of the inner workings of expansions and recessions, and you are aware of investor psychology. You are now prepared to join the **SMART**est investors who know how to stay ahead of the curve, taking advantage of expanding economic growth, minimizing risk by knowing when to sell, and getting back into the market at the right time.

CHAPTER SIX

Fine Tuning Your Asset Allocation *to* Maximize Wealth

PROFITING FROM BULL AND BEAR MARKETS

" Wealth is the ability to fully experience life.
—*Henry David Thoreau* "

WE KNOW FROM HISTORY THAT A static asset allocation plan doesn't work. That is the equivalent of modern portfolio theory where you simply take a "set it and forget it" approach to managing a portfolio. This method assumes that a broadly diversified portfolio will balance out gains and losses among many classes of investments during both expansionary and recessionary markets.

As we have seen, however, today's global markets are chaotic and interconnected. Markets can be hit hard by sudden events no matter where in the world they happen. The key to **SMART** investing is therefore to use an "active asset allocation" approach based on studying and understanding where we are in the economic cycle. By assessing whether the market is in a recovery and moving into an expansion, or whether it is about to peak and begin its descent into a recession, the **SMART**est investors strategically adjust their exposure to the stock market.

- When the market is on the upswing, you increase your stock market allocation towards the maximum level of your risk tolerance according to your ROR.

- When the market is on the downswing, you reduce your stock market exposure towards the minimum level of your ROR.

Active asset allocation thus helps you take advantage of the profit potential in an expanding market or minimize losses in a falling market.

Anyone can learn to perform the same process of active asset allocation that I follow in my practice. This chapter will teach you the specific techniques I use and some important rules I follow.

PRINCIPLE II

BUSINESS FUNDAMENTALS ARE MORE IMPORTANT THAN EMOTIONS

The most basic asset allocation "action" guideline is to increase your stock exposure at the beginning of an expanding business cycle and reduce your stock exposure as the cycle matures and moves towards a recession. You must take into account the timing of the cycle, as well as the strength of its peaks and valleys. As you will learn in this chapter, you can also adjust the groups and types of stocks in your stock portfolio to further enhance your returns and manage risk.

First Determine Where We Are in the Business Cycle

Many factors will signal the current status

As you learned in the last chapter, economic cycles follow a pattern of five stages. Each stage of the economic cycle has varying and significant effects on stocks, bonds, real estate, currencies, etc. For instance, during recessions or contractions, stock prices fall dramatically while bond prices tend to rise significantly. An understanding of what stage of the business cycle the economy is experiencing is a key component to managing investment return and risk. To invest without the business cycle in mind is hazardous to your wealth.

This has significant implications for investors who are trying to determine where in a cycle the economy is. It would be great if Wall Street all agreed that we were in a certain stage, or if an economist in the government would make a public announcement to warn investors. But such clarity never happens. Investors are pretty much left to themselves to decide what stage the economy is in and whether a transition to the next phase is coming soon.

This is a very difficult task requiring sophisticated forecasting tools that monitor the rate of change of everything from gross domestic product (GDP) growth to industrial production indexes and consumer confidence data. A well-conceived forecast of the business cycle allows investors to prepare their portfolios to generate returns and more importantly manage risk.

In general, I like to examine a variety of measures to get a picture of where we are in the economic cycle, not just in the United States but around the world. First off, I continually watch the leading indicators of business: unemployment rate, GDP, industrial production, consumer confidence, home foreclosures, and other concrete economic measures. When the majority of these start

to decline, it is likely that a recession is on the way. On the other hand, if these indicators remain stable or rise slightly, it means that the current period of recovery or expansion will continue.

Other signals to study

In addition, I study many additional statistical measures to gain even greater clarity on the business cycle, including the following:

- **Interest Rate Policy.** Every government helps to set interest rates. Banks borrow money at these interest rates and loan those funds to businesses. In the US, the Federal Reserve Board determines our interest rate policy. Checking FRB announcements every few months (or immediately if necessary) is a good way to get a sense if the economy is speeding up or slowing down. If the FRB raises interest rates, it usually indicates that they believe the economy is expanding too rapidly. If the FRB lowers interest rates, it reflects a belief that the economy has slowed too much and needs stimulus. Thus, interest

rate policy is often a good predictor of what stage the government believes the business cycle is in.

- **Inflation.** As discussed earlier, inflation varies each year due to a number of factors, and causes the value of money to shrink. Inflation can occur when consumer and business demand for products exceeds supply, and companies raise their prices. Competition for housing and energy can also cause inflation. When inflation occurs, it puts pressure on salaries as workers need more to live on. When inflation is increasing, it usually means the economy is heating up. When inflation falls, it usually means the economy is falling. Watching the rate of inflation is a clue to where we are in the economic cycle.

- **Stock Market Price /Earnings Ratio.** The stock market price-to-earnings ratio (P/E) looks at the average price of shares across a segment of the entire stock market (such as the S&P 500), divided by the

average earnings of companies. If the average P/E ratio is heading up, it usually reflects a rising economy. If it is declining, it may indicate that a recession is on the way.

- **Asset Valuation Model (also known as Fed Model).** This is a tremendously useful statistical model that compares the stock market's earnings yield (E/P, which is not the same as the P/E) to the yield on long-term government bonds. The theory is that when the 1-year forward-looking E/P of stocks equals the 10-year Treasury note yield, it means that the stock and bond markets are in equilibrium. This model helps us measure the attractiveness of stocks compared to other asset classes. For instance, if the stock market's earnings yield is higher than the government bond yield, it means investors should shift their money into stocks.

- **Trends evidenced by investor psychology.** Clues about the business cycle can often be obtained by watching the stock market and what investors are doing. One indication, for example, is when it is clear that investors are overly exuberant, overbidding and overvaluing stocks. This shows that investors have priced in all of the "good news" in regard to the economic cycle. It is usually the period when the mood of the average investor is overly optimistic and making money in the markets seems easy. Think 1999 or 2007. This period of overvaluation is usually what precedes bear markets and the ugly math that comes with them.

By using these statistical measures related to the business cycle as a guide—not emotions or what someone said on CNBC—I adjust a portfolio's exposure to stocks in a manner that will be beneficial no matter where we are in an economic cycle. This process keeps your stock exposure within the boundary of the original asset allocation blueprint, but takes it a step further by reducing and changing the stock market exposure as the economic cycle ages.

The Game Plan When Signals Point to a Recovery and Expansion

How to ride the bull and enjoy it!

We know that economic expansions are great for stocks in general, given the correlation between growing economies and rising corporate profits during these periods. We also know from history that the average expansion in recent decades lasts for 7 to 9 years.

Here are the fundamental guidelines I follow when deciding what to do with investments when the signals clearly show a recovery starting.

1 Year 0: If a recession has just ended within the last year, the odds are that stocks in general will start an upward bias. I therefore would slowly start to increase the asset allocation to have a greater exposure to the stock market, buying stocks that will benefit from an expanding economy.

2 Years 1 to 4: If there is definitive evidence of an economic expansion and it's in its early years, I would push stock exposure to the highest level the investor can tolerate. The rationale for this is that as the economy grows, more people become employed, wages increase, businesses sell more products and services, and profits in general increase. It is during this stage of the economic cycle that stock prices tend to rise, reflecting the underlying earnings growth of the companies that they represent. The corresponding rise of stock prices transforms this period into a bull market you don't want to miss.

3 Years 5 to 7: Depending on the signals, I may continue to retain that maximum exposure but begin changing the kind or groups of stocks invested in because different industries fare better at different times during an expansion. I will discuss this in detail later in the chapter.

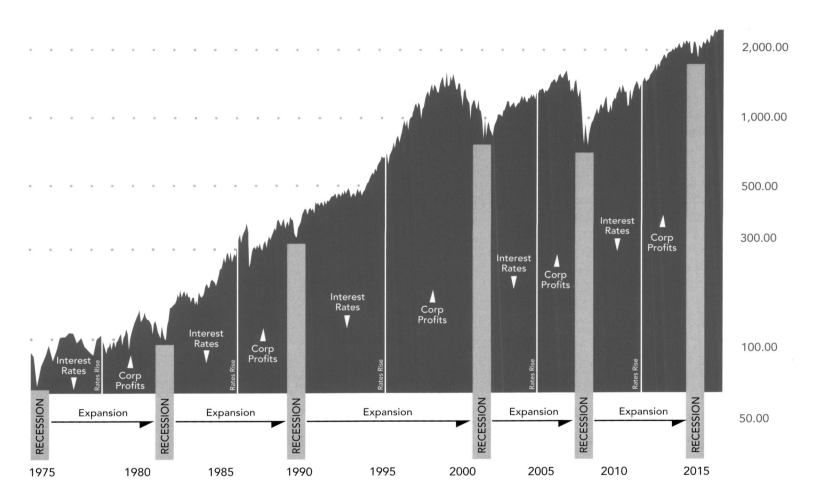

2,000.00

1,000.00

500.00

300.00

Interest
Rates
▼

Corp
Profits
▲

100.00

Interest
Rates
▼

Corp
Profits
▲

Interest
Rates
▼

Corp
Profits
▲

Interest
Rates
▼

Corp
Profits
▲

Interest
Rates
▼

Corp
Profits
▲

Interest
Rates
▼

Corp
Profits
▲

RECESSION   Expansion   RECESSION   Expansion   RECESSION   Expansion   RECESSION   Expansion   RECESSION   Expansion   RECESSION

Rates Rise   Rates Rise   Rates Rise   Rates Rise   Rates Rise

50.00

1975   1980   1985   1990   1995   2000   2005   2010   2015

In the beginning of an expansion, and through years 1– 4, interest rates tend to fall so businesses can borrow more to fund their growth.
Consumers buy more so corporate profits rise. Watch the signals, however, starting in year 5 to see if the expansion will continue or collapse.

Fine Tuning Your Asset Allocation to Maximize Wealth

4 **Year 7+:** If it has been 7 years since the last recession, it's time to be cautious and reduce one's exposure to stocks gradually. Using a methodical process for instance, you might begin selling off those companies that are likely to get hit the hardest. (Later in this chapter, I will discuss how I determine

which companies these could be.) This re-allocation helps maximize gains and prevent serious losses as the market slowly descends or even crashes. From year 7 on, investors should own less in stocks and diversify what stocks they have. This offers protection from an oncoming recession.

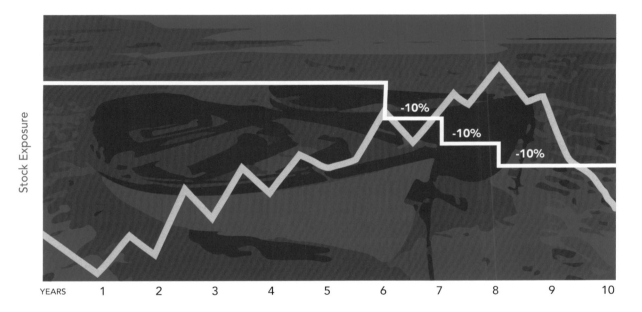

This chart shows how to invest when you identify an expansion about to happen.
Increase your exposure in the stock market for Years 1–5, then depending on the signals,
begin decreasing your exposure by 10% in Years 6–9, ahead of the oncoming recession.

Two Psychological Truths about Bull Markets

Fear and greed—the bookends of investing psychology

Fear and greed are potent motivators. When both of these forces push in the same direction, virtually no human being can resist.

—ANDREW WEIL

Fear: the first truth. What novice investors either don't know or forget is that a bull market is characterized by fear and indecision. Investor optimism about stocks during the early and middle stages of a bull market is usually clouded by the bad experiences they just had in the prior bear market. Investors are usually hesitant to invest in equities for fear the bear market will not truly end or another unexpected crash will occur. This creates an emotional tug-of-war between their fear of losing wealth versus greed that they might miss out on higher returns. Unfortunately, fear usually wins out and tends to keep most investors sidelined during a bull market.

I often ask why investors seem to repeat this same mistake when it comes to investing early enough in bull markets. One theory I have is that recessions only come every 7–9 years and perhaps many people forget the fabulous returns recoveries provide. Another suspicion is that successive generations of new investors, who tend to be younger, did not have enough money to invest in the last cycle and so are unaware of the great returns that can be had by investing at the beginning of an expansion. Though both theories probably play a role, my ultimate view is that most investors just do not pay attention to the business cycle. They have no idea how long

PRINCIPLE 12

DON'T LET FEAR OVERRIDE THE LOGIC OF AN UPWARD TRENDING MARKET

The years of rebound after a recession or downturn offer the greatest opportunity for SMART investors to be in the stock market. If you are thinking of investing, you must be in the market in the first years of a rebound, as this is very likely the start of the next bull market.

expansions can last, and have no tools to measure it even if they did. What a shame!

Ironically, this type of crowd behavior is exactly what you, as a **SMART** investor, need. Why? Because those nervous investors will sell you their stocks at the bottom of a recession when prices are ridiculously cheap. Later on, when these same investors re-enter the market, they will be eager to buy stocks from you when you are selling near the height of the business cycle—so *you* can be the one who realizes the profits and can protect yourself from the collapse when the rising business cycle ends and begins to fall again.

The takeaway from this discussion is the next principle.

Greed: the second truth. Investors often regard bull markets as days of wine and roses. However, their perceptions are warped. By the latter stages of a bull market, they are finally convinced there is indeed a bull market underway and that it will never end. They invest like there is no tomorrow and end up with a portfolio overexposed to equities. Just as you need to enter a bull market as early as possible, you also need to admit that it's important to phase out of a bull market as soon as you see the bear approaching.

Rebalance your Portfolio

If you increased your portfolio in a bull market, those stocks you invest in will begin to pay off through appreciation and dividends that might be reinvested to purchase more stock (which I do not recommend for the reasons explained here). If you invested correctly, your portfolio could therefore soon become over-weighted in your exposure to equities, as your investment in stocks becomes an increasingly larger share of your entire portfolio. Be sure to watch your portfolio for this and make adjustments by selling shares or adjusting your stock choices.

Take our hypothetical Dr. Thomas, who needed a 6% return. If he had a 50% stake in equities throughout the expansion, it is entirely possible that his exposure could grow to 60% or even 70% of his entire portfolio. From time to time, he must trim back the portfolio to maintain the 50% ratio of equities to his other investments. Allowing a portfolio to have excess equity exposure for a short period is fine. However, it should not exceed 10–15% of the target limit. Beyond that, it should be adjusted.

The Game Plan When Signals Point to a Recession

How to run from the bear and get away with your life

Just as I reallocate someone's exposure when signals point to a recovery and expansion, I initiate strategic asset reallocation steps as soon as the signals tell me that an expansion may be hitting its peak and a recessionary period will likely begin.

If you follow the business cycle yourself, you need to be able to notice when a bull market is about to transform into a bear. It is during the contraction and trough phases of the economic cycle that stocks suffer more than nearly every other financial instrument. As companies sell less products and services, and workers become unemployed, corporate profit growth stalls and begins to recede. Since earnings drive stock prices, this translates into declining stock markets.

There are three classic signs suggesting a bear market is nearing. These signs are:

- **The Fed tightens credit too much.**
  Historically, bull markets didn't end when the Fed *starts* to tighten credit. Rather, they ended *after* the Fed tightened it too much. A classic indicator that the Fed has tightened credit too much is an "inverted" yield curve, i.e., short-term loan rates are higher than long-term rates.

- **Stocks are significantly overvalued.**
  If the price-to-earnings ratio of most stocks surpasses their historical highs, it means that investors have overvalued stocks relative to their returns. This often happens when investors enter a bull market in its final years, and competition bids up prices. A lot of overvalued P/E numbers can indicate that the market is about to peak and a bear market will soon set in.

- **Many economic indicators can foretell an oncoming bear market.** Some of these are as obvious as the lights of an oncoming train—reduced GDP, lower production, a decline in housing starts, decreased consumer confidence, declines in the economies of nations closely linked to the US economy, and more. If you see these indicators declining, you will likely be able to spot a market downturn well in advance of other investors.

As we saw earlier, the bear markets of recent history (since WWII) have not lasted as long as expansions. The average length of recessions is now 11.8 months. In that context, here is the four step Active Risk Management (ARM) process I live by when the signals indicate a bear market approaching. These steps will help you minimize your exposure to the bulk of a downturn, thus preserving your assets at the highest level possible.

Step 1: Begin selling into strength.
Trim stocks that have risen in price. This may seem counterintuitive, but since you already made a profit on those companies, it is likely that their rising prices will not last much longer. In the 7th year of an expansion, for example, I sell 10% of the stock portfolio. After that I sell another 10% every year or when the portfolio goes up by 10%—whichever comes first.

Step 2: Create a defensive portfolio.
Sell more of the stocks that appear to be the most vulnerable to a recession first, such as technology stocks, industrial, consumer discretionary, and companies whose products will begin to see declining sales first. Companies that produce consumer necessities are usually the last to experience declines since consumers must continue purchasing their items even in a recession.

Step 3: Diligently keep "stop loss" orders on your stocks. These are automated instructions you leave with your brokerage house to sell a stock the moment it declines to a certain price. I recommend that in a declining market, you sell any stock that declines more than its "normal" fluctuation from its average high over a 4-month period. That way, you protect your initial investment should the stock tumble precipitously on

any given day. You can put automated stop loss orders in and keep revising them as the stock climbs higher over time. I will go into detail about stop loss orders in chapter 8.

Step 4: Let go fully when the market is clearly declining. Don't let your emotions get in the way. Keep your head about you. It is easy to become falsely optimistic that the market will recover soon. But you need to focus on the factual signs of a declining market and admit at the right time that it is about to tank. Don't hold onto a dying portfolio. Divest nearly everything by letting the stop loss orders sell for you or initiating sell orders on your own. Only consider hanging on to consumer staples, utilities, and healthcare stocks as these categories seldom decline much.

These four steps will help protect your wealth. They reflect the exact strategy I use in my practice to maintain the profits earned while the market was rising. The moment I begin to see the signs of an impending decline coalesce, I take these four steps and continue monitoring the market daily to recognize when it is necessary to take each consecutive next step.

The Greatest Bull and Bear Markets of History

There have been numerous fantastic bull markets and bear markets in the past century, both of which had a tremendous impact on investors, as the graphics below show. Many investors who were in these markets grew their wealth in leaps and bounds during the bulls, or lost their shirts (and possibly their homes) during the bears. My hope is that this book will give you the knowledge and confidence to determine when to enter the bull market—and when to exit it.

BULL MARKETS
1920–1929
1950–1958
1990–1999
2002–2007
2009–?

BEAR MARKETS
1929–33
1960
1973–74
1983
1987
2002
2007–09

This list is a reminder that investing in stocks can be enormously profitable. In some of these bull markets, often lasting as much as nine years, increases across all sectors meant that just about any investment would have made a hearty profit.

This list is a reminder that investing in stocks is risky. Declines of the magnitude that occurred during the Great Depression beginning in 1929 and the Great Recession beginning in 2007 can decimate a financial plan and take years to recover from.

Asset Reallocation Using Sector Investing

Another SMART way to use the economic cycle to make money

This section focuses on an important corollary strategy I use to enhance stock portfolio returns and mitigate risk as I perform asset reallocation.

Every economic cycle is a little different, which makes selecting which stocks to put into portfolios challenging as the economic cycle goes through stages. However, there is an interesting pattern of consistency that occurs during every economic cycle that can enhance the performance of your asset reallocation and ward off risk.

This pattern shows that certain types or groups of businesses nearly always perform similarly during specific stages of the business cycle. Their movements are highly correlated with the stages of the economic cycle. For example, in a recession or a slow growing economy, health-care companies still tend to grow their profits and their stocks perform well. Regardless of the economy people get sick and consume health-care products. Meanwhile, industrial companies tend to experience slower profit growth—since their profits are more dependent on economic growth—and their stocks perform poorly.

I like to take advantage of this consistent pattern when I reallocate a portfolio in response to the progressive stages of the business cycle. Called "sector investing," I closely monitor such indicators as GDP, inflation rate, consumer confidence, P/E ratios, and others and select types of stocks whose performance is positively correlated with that stage of the business cycle. Research has shown that investing in sectors during the right economic conditions provides greater potential for returns than investing in stocks generally identified as growth or value stocks. A "sector rotation" strategy minimizes risk, enhances return, and adds value to selecting individual stocks rather than selecting stocks solely on an individual basis.

The 10 Sectors and Their Correlation to the Business cycle

Knowing which sectors perform best during each stage of the business cycle

The Dow Jones Company divides the stock market into 10 basic sectors, which comprise approximately 95% of the US market capitalization, i.e., nearly all stocks of publicly-traded companies. The chart here lists all 59 industry groups that make up the 10 sectors.

CONSUMER DISCRETIONARY

Auto Components

Automobiles

Household Durables

Leisure Equipment & Products

Textiles & Apparel

Hotels, Restaurants & Leisure

Media

Distributors

Internet & Catalog Retail

Multiline Retail

Specialty Retail

CONSUMER STAPLES

Food & Drug Retailing

Beverages

Food Products

Tobacco

Household Products

Personal Products

ENERGY

Energy Equipment & Services

Oil & Gas

FINANCIALS

Banks

Diversified Financials

Insurance

Real Estate

HEALTH CARE

Health Care Equipment & Supplies

Health Care Providers & Services

Biotechnology

Pharmaceuticals

INDUSTRIALS

Aerospace & Defense

Building Products

Construction & Engineering

Electrical Equipment

Industrial Conglomerates

Machinery

Trading Companies & Distributors

Commercial Services & Supplies

Air Freight & Couriers

Airlines

Marine

Road & Rail

Transportation & Infrastructure

INFORMATION TECHNOLOGY

Internet Software & Services

IT Consulting & Services

Software

Communications Equipment

Computers & Peripheral

Electronic Equipment & Instruments

Office Electronics

Semiconductor Equipment & Products

MATERIALS

Chemicals

Construction Materials

Containers & Packaging

Metals & Mining

Paper & Forest Products

TELECOMMUNICATION SERVICES

Diversified Telecommunications

Wireless Telecommunications

UTILITIES

Electric Utilities

Gas Utilities

Multi-Utilities

Water Utilities

Each of these sectors follows, on average, a highly predictable cycle of stock increases and declines, according to various factors that affect the profitability of the companies in that sector. The key is to understand what factors tend to cause a sector to rise or fall. From my experience, I ascribe sector movements to these key influencers:

- **General economic conditions.** Many sectors are sensitive to the general domestic economic condition, such as whether we are experiencing high inflation, stagnation, or are in a recession or a recovery.

- **Consumer confidence and purchasing power.** Many sectors are directly affected by whether consumers have money to spend and are optimistic about the future.

- **Supply and demand for business goods.** Many sectors are tied into supplying goods and services to businesses; a rising economy feeds their profits, while a declining economy takes a toll on their profits.

- **Politics.** The political climate impacts sectors to the extent that new regulations and tax laws might influence an industry. Stocks can even react to expectations about which party might win an election.

- **New technology.** Many sectors are positively impacted when new technology is

PRINCIPLE 13

USING SECTORS TO CHOOSE INDUSTRIES BUT NOT INDIVIDUAL STOCKS

Analyzing sectors can offer insights when you evaluate potential performance in the context of the economic cycle. However, understanding which sectors may rise and which decline in the coming quarters does not guarantee that any single company stock within that sector will follow what the sector does. Before selecting a stock to buy when reallocating your portfolio, choose an industry, research the top performing companies in that industry, and do some "fundamental analysis" on them. The tools of fundamental analysis are presented in the next chapter.

created that lower their costs, make their operations more efficient, or increase profitability.

- **Domino effect.** Some sectors rise after another sector rises, because the companies in that sector depend on the profitability of the other sector.

- **Global political and financial events.** Some sectors are highly influenced by global affairs.

This is not to say that every company within a sector rises and falls exactly in tandem with others as the sector moves. Investors still value each company separately, depending on its underlying fundamentals. Any single company in a sector can be an anomaly and do poorly relative to other firms in the same sector. But as a general rule, a rising sector tends to lift most boats in that sector. In this way, investing in a sector at the right moment when all signs point to its ascendancy gives investors a leg up on the market.

Taking into account these factors, let's look at how sectors historically behave in the business cycle, as the chart on the next page shows.

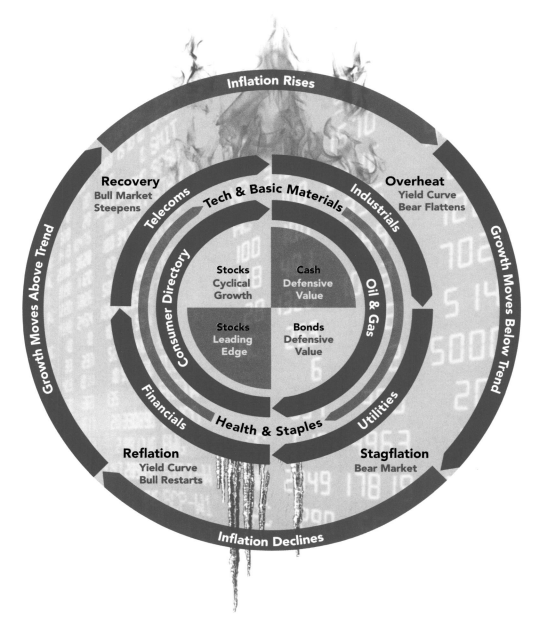

Here's how to read the chart. Based on the assumption the economy is starting a recovery, I will explain the chart moving clockwise, beginning in the upper left corner.

Upper left corner: Assume the market is beginning a recovery. As the economy begins heating up, stocks tend to experience a cyclical growth curve up, while commodities rise on cyclical value. In such a market, stocks like telecoms, industrials, tech and basic materials, and consumer discretionary purchases usually rise as the economy improves. Consumers and businesses need goods and services, and as higher sales lead to higher production and higher employment, it creates a positive feedback loop.

Upper right corner: As growth tends to fuel inflation and the economy overheats, investors begin pulling back on stocks. This triggers a downturn, which impacts many consumer and industrial sectors. As the business cycle slows, with less output and production, the industrial sector slows too. This reduces the need for energy (oil and gas), pushing those stocks down. This is when investors should be taking their money out of the stock market, holding it mostly in defensive sectors and cash.

Lower right corner: Next in a typical business cycle, the economy hits bottom, finally halting inflation. Consumers continue to purchase mostly staples and pharmaceuticals that fulfill their basic needs. Investors, still wary of a nascent market that remains in the doldrums, tend to take a defensive position by putting their money into bonds, which have higher returns than cash.

Lower left corner: To complete the cycle, a bull market starts again, as the economy once again improves. Investors return to put their money into the leading edge of recovery stocks—industrials, energy, financials, telecoms, and technology, as these sectors have traditionally been the first to see profit growth in the early months of a rebound.

The cycle then continues back around again over the next business cycle that may last 7 to 9 years.

Business Cycles and the Relative Sector Performance

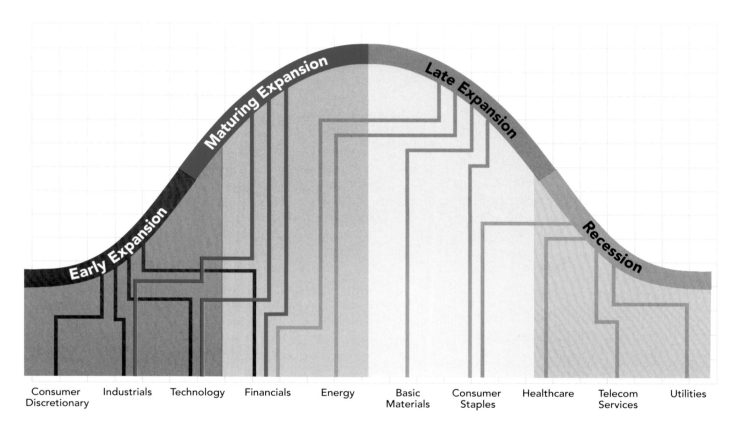

This graphic shows when stocks in each of 10 leading sectors tend to perform the best. However, each company within a sector must be evaluated individually, as not all stocks within a sector perform equally.

Steps to Buying Sector Stocks at the Right Time

History proves it works

There are many brokerage houses that offer sector-based mutual funds and exchange-traded funds (ETFs), in which the fund is entirely devoted to investing in only a specific sector such as industrials, energy, or biotechnology. However, my position is that investing directly in individual stocks in a rising sector is a **SMART**er strategy. I believe that choosing specific companies based on their performance and fundamentals provides investors with the potential for better returns and less risk than a broad-based sector mutual fund or ETF that likely contains as many losers as winners—to say nothing about the extra management fees involved. On average, mutual funds, even sector-based ones, do not yield the returns that a well-chosen individual stock can.

A Caveat about Robo-Investing (Part 1)

Latest trends in investing

One of the latest trends in investing is "robo-investing," which uses technology to automate trading for you, usually in mutual funds or ETFs. Many brokerage houses and wealth management firms are now offering robo-investing and promoting this service as a less expensive alternative to mutual fund companies or fees for a wealth management firm.

We do not recommend robo-investing because you are not investing directly in stocks, as discussed here. Also, robo advice is advertised as free or at a low management fee, but it actually employs exchange traded or index funds that charge on average 44 basis points (or 0.44%) annually—hardly free. Lastly, robo-investing does not offer the risk management protections that you will read about in Chapter 8.

Here are the steps I recommend when you want to buy stocks to reallocate your portfolio using sector analysis:

1

First, consider where we are in an economic cycle. If it is not clear to you what phase the economy is in, do some research to identify what financial analysts say about the condition of the economy. Look at the common indicators of economic growth, such as GDP, inflation, consumer confidence, and recent stock market history.

2

Next, select one or more sectors that are likely to experience growth in the future based on the economic conditions. Always look to the future, not to the past, as you size up which sector(s) might perform well in coming months, correlated to the economic cycle.

3

Research companies in that sector using fundamental analysis, as explained in the following chapter.

4

Finally, identify potential risks that might impact the sector and the stock(s) you have selected: rising inflation, increasing unemployment, higher gas and oil prices, loss of consumer confidence, political turmoil, and other factors. Watch for any changes in the economy that could create the conditions for these risks to occur, and be prepared to sell the stock should it begin to fall below your threshold of tolerance.

How Fast Is This Expansion Running

Take a look at the speedometer!
Identifying what part of the economic cycle you are in is important to be a **SMART** investor, but it is also important to assess at what rate the economy is growing. Faster growing economies favor certain kinds of companies, while slow economies favor others. The best way to measure economic growth is to review GDP numbers in the US and overseas. The last four quarters are helpful for two reasons. First, they help you obtain an average rate of growth for the past year. This will tell you if the economy is growing faster or slower than normal. For instance, in the US a 2–3% growth rate has become "normal."

The second reason to use the last four quarters is that they act as a barometer for understanding whether the rate of change of economic growth is accelerating or decelerating. Economic expansions that are accelerating can greatly benefit certain sectors and vice versa. So be sure to check the rate of speed of the economic expansion.

159

The "speedometers" of the US and Chinese economy reflect significant differences. The US GDP tends to rise at 2–3% annually, while the Chinese GDP has now slowed to 7% from its former supercharged high over 10% annually.

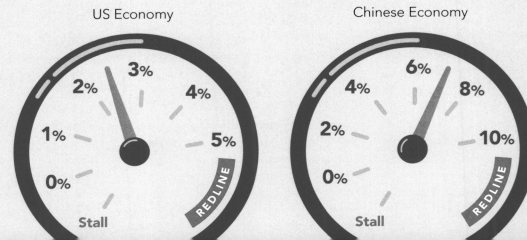

US Economy

Chinese Economy

Sector Performance in 2011–2016

What we can learn from history in evaluating sectors

Correlating sectors to economic conditions has proven to be extremely valuable in predicting performance. The chart shows the performance of the top 10 sectors in the five-year period from 2011–2016, during which the economy was in recovery from the 2008 recession.

Stock Sectors: Total Returns (%)

Sector Name	1-Year	3-Year	5-Year
Basic Materials	13.47%	7.90%	48.35%
Telecom Services	22.54%	25.31%	65.87%
Consumer Discretionary	4.14%	21.80%	108.61%
Consumer Staples	1.27%	20.40%	59.15%
Energy	25.42%	-14.07%	8.95%
Financials	18.95%	31.64%	120.25%
Healthcare	-5.14%	24.28%	98.73%
Industrials	16.51%	9.76%	84.35%
Technology	12.91%	35.31%	90.01%
Utilities	11.01%	28.15%	34.99%

We can deduce two conclusions from this chart:

- **Best 5-year returns.** Looking at the five-year returns from 2011 to 2016, financials, consumer discretionary, and healthcare had the highest total returns, while energy, utilities and basic materials fared the poorest. These results show how, in coming out of the Great Recession, consumer demand for healthcare, financial services, and consumer spending led investor gains. It was an era of great improvement in healthcare research and biotech as well as advances in technology. As the economy grew during that period consumer spending on discretionary items such as homes and cars was robust. However, the depth of the 2008 recession took a major toll on utilities, energy and basic materials which struggled to recover during the powerful 2011–2016 stock market rally that boosted other sectors.

- **Best one-year returns.** The one-year returns are also revealing. We can see that between 2015 and 2016, as the economy transitioned from the mild corporate profit recession, the sectors of energy, telecom, and financial stocks retained the top positions. This reflects the recovery of the banks and the build-up of investor wealth that had been fueling an upward swing of financial stocks. Healthcare, staples and consumer discretionary fared the worst. For healthcare, this was the result of the controversy over pharmaceutical pricing which weighed heavily on the drug makers. As for the poor performance of staples and consumer discretionary stocks during the period, the transition from corporate profit recession to recovery made these sectors a mixed bag of results. The staples gave up their gains as the economy stabilized, while the consumer discretionary companies declined during the economies rough patch.

Wide diversification is only required when investors do not understand what they are doing.
—WARREN BUFFETT

The Evergreen Sectors: Food, Shelter, Healthcare

Food, shelter and healthcare are necessities. Their industries tend to be evergreen investments. Whether the economy is doing well or not, stocks in these companies usually remain stable, with consistently good to moderate growth over time. This appears to remain true whether there is global political stability and rising GDPs, or political instability and stagnation. The more that countries lift their populations into the middle class, the more investors can count on these three sectors to show exceptional growth.

During the horrific bear market of 2008 Proctor & Gamble shares actually rose, while most stock indexes declined by over 50%. Why? Investors recognized that consumers would continue to buy P&G's products (Tide detergent and Crest toothpaste among others) regardless of the economic recession and that P&G's profits would hold up, justifying a stable stock price.

The Discipline of Asset Allocation and Sectors

The first steps to getting control of your investment decisions

The active asset allocation presented in this chapter removes the human brain from its age old game of preventing us from doing what's right for our financial success. It's never easy investing after a recession when stocks have been clobbered. The media makes it even worse by telling us that the "sky is falling" and the world will never be the same. Therefore, the only **SMART** way to handle these periods of time is to initiate and follow a process and a discipline that have stood the test of time. Turn down the sound on CNBC, remember that the crowd and their perspective is usually wrong (and often the opposite of what a prudent investor should do), and follow a disciplined strategy that works.

Along with asset reallocation, being savvy about correlating your sector exposure with the business cycle are the two winning steps to **SMART** investing to maximize a bull market and mitigate the risk of a bear market. I highly suggest that you pay attention to the 10 sectors in the global equity market and follow them through the economic cycles. Sector investing can greatly simplify your choice of stock investments—and provide you with the greatest returns while minimizing your risks.

CHAPTER SEVEN

How *to* Select Individual Stocks *to* Grow Wealth

WHAT TO DO AFTER YOU KNOW YOUR ROR, ASSET ALLOCATION AND SECTOR INVESTING

> " If you want to have a better performance than the crowd, you must do things differently from the crowd.
>
> —*John Templeton* "

YOU NOW KNOW THE FUNDAMENTALS of using stocks to grow wealth. I discussed the importance of having an individualized ROR that helps determine an appropriate asset allocation blueprint that makes sense for your risk profile. We then looked at how the business cycle affects the stock market, moving in a regular pattern to create cycles of bull and bear markets. Lastly, you learned about my strategic process of active asset allocation based on the business cycle.

Now I will explain how to decide which stocks to purchase for your portfolio. Novice investors tend to follow their whims, listen to recommendations from friends, or read newspapers and magazines for tips when picking stocks. I recommend a precise strategic process for selecting stocks. The first step of this process is determining which stage of the business cycle we are in. This determination is made by researching and paying close attention to the economic signals. Once the business cycle stage is identified, you can be more knowledgeable in determining how to allocate or reallocate your portfolio to increase or decrease your exposure to the stock market.

The goal is then to find the stocks that will yield the highest returns in the current and future stages of the business cycle. The problem is, there are over 100,000 publicly traded stocks in the world, though most of them are not worth looking at, much less investing in. How can you identify which stocks will perform the best?

It would be very time-consuming to evaluate thousands of domestic and international stocks. I therefore look first at the various sectors, as discussed in the last chapter. Given that the sectors are highly correlated with the business cycle, this helps you begin choosing which stocks to evaluate further.

Selecting stocks that will likely have the best performance is the first step of elimination, but it still leaves thousands of potential stock choices in each sector to evaluate. How can investors find the most winning stocks among so many choices and sectors? This chapter describes the advanced tools I use to make decisions about which specific stocks to buy, a process that is also critical in determining the best timing for buying and selling.

You can follow this process on your own, but it requires time, experience, patience, a willingness to learn, and a commitment to conduct rigorous research. The process makes the job of selecting stocks easier, but it can still be a perplexing and challenging endeavor.

An investment in knowledge pays the best interest.
—BENJAMIN FRANKLIN

Using Fundamental Analysis to Select Stocks
The big seven fundamental analysis tools

Once you select a sector or group of stocks, your goal is to find those that are generating the highest returns and are likely to continue performing well in the future. This requires comparing the performance of many companies using the advanced tools of "fundamental analysis" to evaluate the potential value of a stock and its current pricing through underlying company financial data. This process considers many variables directly related to the company without regard to the stock market overall or the sector or industry group in which it operates.

I use seven key fundamental analysis tools to assess a company's business, determine whether its underlying stock is currently undervalued, overvalued or fairly priced, and evaluate its growth potential. Graham and Dodd, Warren Buffett, John Templeton, Peter Lynch and other top investors embrace fundamental analysis and achieve enviable long-term results. Peter Lynch of Fidelity Investments often said that he paid little attention to the overall direction of the stock market in his investment decisions, but rather to the fundamentals of a company.

You don't need to create these fundamental analysis tools yourself. Many Wall Street companies regularly publish the results of their fundamental analyses. All you need to know is how to interpret these tools and use them to screen for the best stocks. I believe that the following stock screening metrics will help you select stocks with higher stock price performance over time, with less risk.

Screening Factor 1: Debt Levels

When companies borrow to expand their business, it is usually based on the premise that their overall business will grow or that a new product will produce greater profits. Taking on long-term debt (debt payable more than one year away) to invest in this growth can accelerate the process by providing the cash for a larger workforce, new infrastructure, or new products launches. In this way, debt is a friend to companies and can enhance profit growth and underlying stock price.

However, CEOs and Boards of Directors can be wrong about the prospects for future business or the success of a new product launch. As we all know, there are plenty of cases of

CEOs who made disastrous decisions, losing their company hundreds of millions of dollars. Bad decisions sometimes reflect executive and board blind spots, but there are also dozens of variables that can derail even the most well-thought-out growth strategies. These include an unexpected economic downturn, a change in government regulations, geopolitical instability, or just a more stagnate consumer environment than anticipated. Many projects take years to develop, and unexpected economic conditions can occur to interfere with the plans of highly intelligent business leaders.

If business plans fail to materialize into profits, a dangerous downward spiral can occur in a company that has significant existing levels of debt. With slowing profits, the burden of servicing the debt becomes magnified and makes the company vulnerable. As opposed to a debt-free company, the slightest negative event can increase the firm's vulnerability and cause it to slash employment, reduce production, and halt new product research—the opposite of what stockholders (particularly institutional investors) want to see.

Of course, this can translate into a falling stock price, which can then prompt more investors to dump the stock. It becomes a vicious cycle for companies with high debt that cannot be paid down. The following is a list of companies that used to lead their industries, but were ruined by excessive debt and some hard-to-predict negative events:

Washington Mutual

US Airways

Bear Stearns

WorldCom

Chesapeake Energy

It is therefore vital to examine a company's debt. Frankly, I prefer companies with zero debt, but I also understand that some economic sectors and industries are very capital intensive and cannot make it without some debt to fund their infrastructure and equipment. If you are considering a company that carries debt on their balance sheet, you want to target those that have less debt than their peers because it means they have greater leverage and less liability that could detract from their profits.

Screening Factor 2: Debt-to-Equity Ratio

Knowing the amount of debt a company has can be invaluable, but sometimes it is difficult to draw a conclusion because debt is just a single number. What does it mean if a company owes $10 million or $50 million in long-term debt? What insight does that give us about its future performance?

That's why it is also useful to measure a company's debt-to-equity ratio. Equity is the total value of all stockholder shares in the company. Like debt, companies use the money from stockholders to invest in their growth, launch new products, hire employees, pay for infrastructure, and so on. If a company has both stockholder equity and debt, it is effectively borrowing money in two ways.

The debt/equity ratio is thus a measure of how much the company holds in debt from creditors versus investment from stockholders. The lower the number, the more the company depends on stockholders' equity rather than debt. For example, if a company has $500 million in long-term debt versus $2 billion in stockholder equity, the ratio is 1 to 4, or 25%. But if the same company has $1 billion in debt, its ratio is 1:2 or 50%, which means that its stockholders are at greater risk should the company be unable to pay its debts.

In general, I do not recommend investing in companies that have debt-equity ratios greater than 30%, unless they are in finance or companies in which debt is part of their business.

Screening Factor 3: Return on Equity (ROE)

The term "return" in the equation of ROE does not refer to how much investors get back, but how much the company as a whole earns in net income compared to the total of shareholder's equity. ROE measures a corporation's profit capability by expressing how much profit the company generates with the money its shareholders have invested. ROE is calculated as a percentage using the following equation:

NET INCOME / SHAREHOLDERS EQUITY = RETURN ON EQUITY

NOTE: When companies calculate net income, they usually do so for the full fiscal year before dividends are paid to common stockholders, but after dividends are paid to preferred stockholders, who have first rights to be paid their dividends.

Companies with a high ROE ratio have strong cash flows because they are generating a high net income. A high ROE means the company is doing well employing its funds to increase shareholder value, such as adding workforce, launching new products, or entering new markets. In my experience, companies with relatively high ROE have a history of successful stock price performance.

The average ROE for the overall stock market is currently 9%. But in the fundamental analysis I like to use, I strive to identify finely-tuned companies that exhibit ROE's of 15% or higher. Historically, many investments have been in firms with ROE's over 20% and even 30%, making them better investments for people, as these unique companies show steadily reliable rising stock prices over time.

Screening Factor 4: Earnings Growth Rate

Earnings are the "bottom line" when it comes to valuing a company's stock. Earnings are defined as the net profit (or loss) a company earns after

What Exactly Are You Calling 'Debt?'

The term debt does not have a fixed definition. Some analysts use only long-term debt when calculating the debt/equity ratio. Others use the total of both long-term and short-term liabilities that the company has. When evaluating a stock based on the debt/equity ratio, be sure to know which definition of debt is being used.

expenses and taxes. Looking at a company's earnings is a highly revealing factor in deciding whether you should invest in that company or not. However, earnings can change quickly. A single year's earnings may be misleading.

That is why analysts prefer to look at the growth of earnings over time. The growth rate of corporate profits is a more useful measure than a single annual report showing the dollar amount of earnings. Companies that have a history of increasing profits, particularly at an above average pace, typically have a history of rising stock prices. In this regard, we again see how the stock market is efficient; it rewards rising earnings with rising stock prices.

As a result, one of my rules in creating a "**SMART** Portfolio" is to focus on companies that have a history of strong earnings growth. This may sound like common sense, but there are many well-known publicly traded companies that have no profits or lose money.

There are some exceptions to this rule, though it is rare for me to invest in these companies. Many younger companies have become popular with investors, despite the fact that they lose money in their first years as they try to establish a market for their product or service. A few of these companies may turn into another Cisco or Google, but most burn up and leave shareholders with a stock trading at "$0.00."

To avoid this, I select companies that generate real earnings. Some of these companies may be young but have recently turned profitable, while others have a long history of earnings growth. In addition, I seek to find companies where earnings growth is trending higher and where management identifies opportunities for the company to accelerate earnings growth, given their business model.

ONE REMINDER: The stock market is also not infallible. There are many instances where investors have ineffectively valued a company based on its earnings. The stock price may have risen or fallen without a positive correlation to the company's recent earnings. Such cases create great opportunities for us to use fundamental analysis to identify companies that could have hidden potential unrecognized by other investors.

Ouch! I paid too much!

The P/E ratio fundamental is one you often hear about because it is a staple of **SMART** investing. Many investors make a common mistake. They buy great companies with good potential, but at too high a price! This is usually a result of chasing the best performing stocks, or the market as a whole, after the bulk of the stock's rise is already over. Such behavior is wired in our psychology—a false optimism that "things that have already gone up will go up some more" as well as plain old-fashioned greed—both of which are the enemy of successful investing.

There are many high performing companies, but it is counterproductive to pay too much to invest in them. The challenge for investors is to isolate those that offer the greatest rewards—and then narrow it down to a select few whose stock price is undervalued relative to the company's earnings. We measure this using the P/E ratio. This formula divides a company's full-year fiscal earnings per share (EPS) by the company's current stock price.

$$\frac{\text{EARNINGS PER SHARE}}{\text{PRICE}}$$

For example, if the large British beverage distributor Diageo's stock is selling at $80 per share and it has an EPS of $8.00 per share, then it has a P/E ratio of 10. This number by itself tells investors how much the market is willing to pay for a company's earnings.

The P/E ratio alone can be revealing about a company. If investors recognize that a company's fundamentals are in poor condition and future earnings problems may be afoot, the stock price will suffer, lowering the P/E. But it can be difficult to assess a company based on its P/E alone. What does the number on its own tell us about the company? We need a context to understand if it is good or bad.

For this reason, the P/E ratio is more valuable when you use it to compare many stocks together, especially stocks in the same industry. If, for example, Diageo is trading at a P/E of 10 and all of its competitors are selling at P/E's of 15, then Diageo would be considered a "value" relative to its peers. If Diageo eventually traded at a P/E of 15, the stock price would have to increase

Two Other Unbeatable Research Tools

The 10-Q and the analysts' conference call
Finding out about corporate earnings is not hard. Every publicly traded company must report their earnings each quarter in a document required by the Securities & Exchange Commission called a 10-Q. These reports, along with the company's annual reports, contain volumes of useful data if you know how to read them.

Furthermore, as a part of your fundamental analysis, it is important to know not just the history of earnings growth through these quarterly reports, but to have a sense of the firm's future earnings growth. This is best done through the quarterly conference calls with management that occur a few weeks after the 10-Q report is published. In these calls, you can gain an understanding of the company's product cycle, industry fundamentals, and management's forward-looking statements about the future.

Conference calls were not formerly open to the public, as they were intended only for Wall Street analysts and institutional investors. But today, more and more companies are allowing investors to listen in on the calls, or to an online stream of the live call, which is recorded and made available for several days after the conference. You can find announcements about upcoming calls on the websites of most companies, along with information on how to listen in or hear the recording.

50%, creating a great profit for the investor who bought into it at $80/share.

Beware, however, that the P/E ratio can be interpreted incorrectly. A low P/E does not necessarily suggest that an investor has found a diamond in the rough—it could reveal a company that is troubled. Similarly, a high P/E could be a one-time event caused by a stock price that recently skyrocketed on a rumor you were unaware of, and that proves to be false. Sometimes stocks that have very high P/E's are very fast-growing companies, whose share prices investors have overvalued in their enthusiasm for its potential growth.

In short, don't take a P/E at face value. You have to do further research to understand the significance of a high P/E. It might be that the company is the right one to buy, or it could reflect that all the good news has already been incorporated into the high P/E.

Screening Factor 6: Price Earnings versus Growth Rate (PEG)

P/E versus Growth (called the PEG rate) is another valuable fundamental as it helps investors project a stock's value into the future. PEG is calculated by taking a stock's P/E ratio and dividing it by its expected percentage earnings growth for the next year.

For example, Company A has a P/E of 20 and expects its earnings to grow 20% next year. Its PEG ratio would be 20/20 = 1. Company B also has a P/E of 20 but a projected earnings growth of 10%, so its PEG would be 20/10 = 2.

Which is better? The first one, because the lower the PEG, the better the value for investors since they are paying less for each unit of earnings growth. A PEG of 1 suggests the stock has a reasonable value, given that the stock is priced in line with its earnings growth rate. But a PEG of 3 suggests that the P/E is very high relative to the underlying earnings growth. Look out below!

A great example of how using PEG could help investors occurred during the latter stages of the Internet bubble in the late 1990s. At this time, many technology companies were selling at PEG ratios of 4, 5, and even 6! This should have been a loud warning bell, but investor expectations had been so elevated that they were bidding up stock prices far beyond any possibility of the underlying earnings ability to catch up. In 2000, the floor fell out of the market for technology stocks when it became clear that these companies had little or no earnings to justify their prices.

This list is a great example of the perils of buying high P/E stocks that had overvalued PEG ratios from 2000 to 2016:

> *Krispy Kreme*
>
> *Nokia*
>
> *Alibaba*
>
> *Sirius XM*
>
> *GoPro*
>
> *Enron*

Screening Factor 7: Price/Sales Ratio

In today's world, new companies go public and sell stock often well in advance of significant earnings. Think Facebook, Twitter, and other social media firms, as well as companies in new biotechnology arenas and other new fields.
In these cases, investors may want to look at the Price/Sales ratio, which compares the stock's price to its current total sales, recognizing that there may be no earnings from these sales given the expenses of the startup. However, knowing the price-to-sales ratio at least becomes a method to benchmark new ventures.

PRINCIPLE 14

FUNDAMENTAL ANALYSIS COMES TO THE RESCUE

The core of fundamental analysis lies in examining seven indicators: 1) debt; 2) debt / equity ratio; 3) return on equity; 4) earnings growth rate; 5) price/earnings ratio; 6) price earnings growth; and 7) price/sales ratio. These seven factors are the leading fundamental analysis indicators that can help you screen stocks based on financial analysis, not emotion, and select the most profitable ones for your portfolio.

Which "Earnings" Are You Referring To?

When you are evaluating the P/E ratios of stocks, beware that analysts may be using different measures. Some use total earnings from the last four quarters (actual) while others use projected earnings over the next four quarters (estimated). The last four quarters are history and are not a useful reflection of where the company is headed. For this reason, most analysts use reasonable future earnings projections when calculating P/E's. Be sure you know what the P/E is based on, and use the same definition for all P/E's that you evaluate.

When it comes to evaluating whether to use past or future earnings, remember what Wayne Gretzky said about hockey:
"Skate to where the puck is going,
not where it has been."

Using Outside Research for a "Second Opinion"

But don't believe everything you read!

If you've used fundamental analysis and sector analysis to select some stocks to purchase, I highly recommend that you double check your results with what others are thinking about each stock. This is where outside research comes in. If you think you found a great stock, it is essential that at least a few other people feel the same way. What makes your stocks go up is other investors buying it after you—that is what pushes the price higher. Therefore, it is important that other investors and analysts feel that your stocks are attractive.

You can find extensive information about stocks from Wall Street analysts on a variety of websites and in business newspapers and magazines. Once you have subdivided your screening results by sector, you can look at a variety of analysts for a second opinion. Many of these research analysts are experts in a specific sector and have studied the companies within it for decades. They can lend significant confirmation or doubt to your vetting process.

A caveat, however: keep in mind that there are individuals whose intent is to encourage naïve investors to put their money into scams. It is not uncommon to find articles extolling companies about to explode with profits, but the information is nothing but exaggeration, hyperbole, and even false rumor. There are predators who lure investors to buy a stock, pumping up its price to a point that the predators can then dump their own shares. And, unfortunately, there are insiders who profit from having knowledge about a company that the public does not have.

Publications from Wall Street professionals and business writers are useful to get second opinions on conclusions you have drawn yourself using fundamental analysis, but be careful about researching stocks in general consumer publications. The latter should only be to educate yourself about the economy and the market, broadening your intelligence and savvy. You should apply fundamental analysis to any company before investing in it.

A Database of Global Stocks

One of the key elements of a **SMART** portfolio is the selection of top performing stocks from anywhere in the world. As the economies of nations more closely integrate—many companies are now global, international, or multinational—there is every reason to consider stocks from any nation, traded on any market, if they offer the best returns on your money.

How does one find out about foreign stocks? I often use the MSCI All Country World Index (ACWI) as a benchmark for investigating and identifying the leading global equity returns. This index is comprised of nearly 2500 companies from 46 countries (with slightly more than half based in the US), representing 55% of the world's market capitalization. I have found that this is the best list to select stocks from, given its broad reach and that it has already excluded much of the undercapitalized, low quality publicly traded stocks. However, the prospect of culling through 2500 stocks is one reason why sometimes investors need professionals to perform such research, as they have the time and expertise to select the top global stocks.

Given the tremendous number of variables and continual changes in company fundamentals such as earnings, sales and product cycles, it is very important to establish clear metrics that will lead to greater stock selection success and higher stock prices. My process of fundamental analysis starts with this large list of stocks and then screens each one for the characteristics and metrics that I believe will lead to that success.

Technology enables investors to continually perform screening and to rank each company based on each metric. Knowledge and experience using these metrics enables the **SMART** investor to take a very long list and narrow it to a shorter one of about 300 companies. You can then take this list of top ranked stocks and divide them into their sectors.

This is a key step, as one can isolate the best companies in the most attractive sectors and invest accordingly. A company can have great fundamentals in and of itself, but be in a very difficult sector or industry that we decide to avoid. Remember that 65% of the performance of stocks is sector-related—not fundamentals. This combination of stock fundamental analysis and sectors is essential to knowing which stocks to embrace and buy, as well as which to avoid or sell.

Technical Analysis—Reading the Charts

One final tool in my toolkit

Technical analysis is yet another means I use to get a perspective on how the market is doing. This methodology utilizes past market data, primarily price and volume, to develop models and trading rules based on factors like the relative strength index (which looks at trading volume), as well as moving averages, regressions, inter-market and intra-market price correlations. One of the most noted elements of technical analysis is the examination of chart patterns. While some analysts denigrate the use of charts, believing that any patterns found are meaningless, even behavioral economics and quantitative analysis use the tool.

Technical analysis can be useful, along with the tools of fundamental analysis described in this chapter, to enhance the likelihood of success. By studying the charts of a certain stock, sector or the whole market, you can better identify trends. When the seven fundamentals and technical analysis are both attractive, it can often make for a winning investment.

PRINCIPLE 15

USE FUNDAMENTAL ANALYSIS TO FIND "HIDDEN VALUES"

In general, your goal is to find "hidden value" in companies that have little debt, low debt/equity ratios, high return on equity (ROE), low P/E's, and low PEG ratios. The fundamental analysis of such companies indicates that they have excellent earning potential, while not being overpriced. Their earnings growth rate proves they have the capability to increase profits year after year, suggesting they are well-managed, with the right strategy to succeed in their industry. Their low P/E ratio, relative to competitors, means that other investors have not yet fully discovered the value embedded in these companies, and have not unreasonably bid up the stock's price. Such stocks are not living "in a market bubble" as many technology stocks were in the past—overpriced due to misplaced investor euphoria and emotion with no basis in fundamental value.

Don't Be a Short-Term Market Timer

Throughout history, individual and institutional investors alike have tried to time the market—buying and selling in short time frames, sometimes within just one day—in an effort to predict the direction of stocks. This is a fool's game, as in the short run, stock markets are ruled mostly by crowd psychology and other unpredictable events. Any short-term success of a day trader has more to do with luck than brains from my perspective.

However, when it comes to longer periods of time—quarters and years—the intelligent investor can uncover important trends that lead to higher stock prices or, even more importantly, see the metrics that suggest stocks could fall precipitously. Adjustments must be regularly made in a portfolio because, to repeat, "buy and hold" does not work. My strategic process of longer term trend analysis can provide greater returns than short-term trading, while mitigating risk. This style of investing allows investors to hold onto investments for longer periods of time (but not forever), which reduces transaction costs and is more tax efficient.

It takes as much energy to wish as it does to plan.
—ELEANOR ROOSEVELT

CHAPTER EIGHT

Optimization *and* Risk Management

THE SAVING GRACE OF STOP LOSS ORDERS—
AN UNDERUTILIZED TOOL

> " The only ones to get hurt on a roller coaster are the jumpers.
>
> —*Paul Harvey* "

INVESTING IS RISKY. THINGS CAN GO terribly wrong with one stock (Chipotle in 2015!) or one sector (oil in 2014!) or the whole market (2008!).

What can you do to mitigate these risks? I believe that a **SMART** investor must put as much time and energy into minimizing risk as maximizing opportunity. By avoiding ugly math, you will be much wealthier as you protect yourself from losing a large amount of your portfolio's value if something happens in the market.

When you use the two risk management tools I've recommended—active asset allocation and sector management—you are already doing a good job at risk management. However, there is one other invaluable tool—stop loss orders. Combined with the first two strategic investing methods, carefully placed stop loss orders will help you create truly proactive risk management—a process that can reduce risk in an individual stock, a whole sector, or the market in general.

When I combine active asset allocation, sector management, and stop loss orders, I call it Active Risk Management.

What Is a Stop Loss Order?

The most underutilized tool in the investor's bag!

A stop loss order is an automatic sell order that you place on any individual stock in your portfolio. If a stock falls to a certain price you have selected, the brokerage company automatically sends a sell order to the exchange to sell the stock. If Facebook shares are at 100, you can tell the brokerage to sell the stock at a predetermined price. Let's say in this case you set the stop loss at 88. If the stock falls to 88, the brokerage will automatically send an order to sell the shares. By placing stop loss orders on the companies that may be vulnerable in a bad market or economy, investors immediately create a disciplined process to mitigate catastrophic loss.

What's a great bonus, too, is that stop loss orders have no cost. That's right, they are free to place.

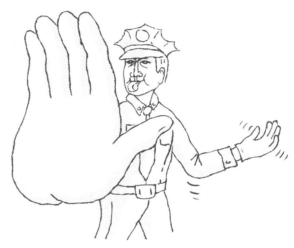

No Stop Loss Orders for Mutual Funds

One of the major disadvantages of investing in mutual funds is that they do not allow you to place stop loss orders. Because they are managed and are valued only once per day (at the end of the day), they are not set up for individual investors to use stop loss orders in the event their price falls.

The Psychology of Why Everyone Needs Stop Loss Orders

The brain is not intended to deal with loss

It is very common for investors to invest in a stock, or a whole sector of the stock market in general, without any tools to manage potential downside. This is because our brains struggle to deal with failure. Even when investing with well-founded research, investors often go into the market with over-optimism. They commonly consider the potential upside, but give little consideration to what can go wrong that can foil a well thought through investment opportunity.

When considering any investment, **SMART** investors must consider potential downside. When stock prices decline, the average investor chalks the movement up to "normal volatility"— which in some cases it very well may be. The little voice in their head says "it will come back" and in some cases it very well may. However, when stock prices continue to fall more than normal, most investors say to themselves, "I'll sell that when it goes back up"—but in many cases it does not. The continued decline para-doxically reinforces their sense of "hope"—the hope that it will come back in value. The little voice says, "I can ride this out." When you are at the stage of "hope" you are at the stock market's mercy, and that is a dangerous and expensive place to be!

Historically, when most stocks, sectors or the stock market in general fall by more than normal, they usually continue to fall further and for a longer period of time. This puts the average investor in a downward psychological spiral that matches the declining value of their investment.

The last stage of the brain's incompetence in handling the stock market is that period when the investment has lost so much value—and ugly math has set in—that it creates hopelessness and the investor no longer can bear to watch or think about it. This is the stage of denial! You don't want to be this investor!

So how can we create a discipline to avoid this common predicament? The lack of a plan to protect the downside is one of the main reasons most investors get poor results. You need to know what you will do if you are wrong about a stock and your investment starts to lose value. You need to have a plan for getting out if the fluctuation in a stock is beyond normal. And you must create a level of discipline to protect yourself from your own optimism.

That's where stop loss orders come in. Along with active asset allocation and sector management, they are a last layer of risk management that you employ to remove the reluctance of the brain to admit failure. This tool silences that voice that tells you to hang on and wait for the value to come back, protecting you from the hopelessness, denial and ugly math that often follows when stocks fall by more than normal.

PRINCIPLE 16
DISCIPLINE YOURSELF TO PUT IN STOP LOSS ORDERS

The use of stop loss orders creates a certain automatic discipline for investors who would not otherwise have it on their own. Let's face it, no one can predict much, if any, of the future in this complex world. No one has ever consistently predicted when bear markets will occur, the decline of a certain sector or the fate of one company. Stop loss orders are a necessary tool to protect us from what we don't know and can't see coming!

On Which Stocks to Place Stop Loss Orders

Two good situations demand them!

You don't need to place stop loss orders on every single one of the stocks in your portfolio, but there are two situations when they are invaluable.

First, stop loss orders are especially valuable in situations when companies have a high likelihood of experiencing an unexpected and unpredictable misfortune or making a grave mistake. You want to have a stop loss order in before other investors suspect a problem.

I can think of countless examples where investors lost fortunes by not using this simple tool when they could have. The market collapses of Enron, Washington Mutual, and Lehman Brothers are all instances when investors lost their entire investment as these companies went bankrupt. The simple use of stop loss orders could have avoided these dire and financially damaging situations.

Stop loss orders are also useful when it comes to sector exposure. If you own stocks in a sector that often experiences wild swings or trouble even though your stock is strong, you can protect yourself against a falling market in that entire sector with a stop loss order. For example, when the technology sector declined catastrophically in 2001–02, investors who had employed stop loss orders could have saved themselves from the hardship of that sector's 70% plunge!

Some sectors, and the stocks within them, hold up fine during recessions since their businesses are immune to economic weakness. But given the disparity of performance of sectors during recessions and bear markets, we can isolate several sectors that necessitate stop loss orders at all times versus those that almost never do.

Stop Loss Orders

Consumer Discretionary

Energy

Financials

Industrials

Materials

Technology

Telecommunication

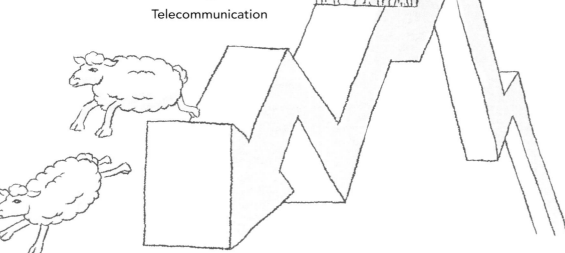

No Stop Loss Orders

Consumer Staples

Healthcare

Utilities

In the graphic on the prior page, history shows that companies in the three industries listed at the bottom produce goods and services that are necessities; regardless of economic conditions, consumers and businesses will consistently purchase from these companies. Investors recognize that the profits for these sectors and companies are thus less likely to be affected by business cycle downturns. As a result, there is less selling in these stocks and they hold up relatively well.

The industries listed at the top of the graphic are another story. Each sector can suffer tremendously in a bear market. Consumers and businesses stop buying these products and services during weak economies. Think auto sales, bank loans, servers and telecom equipment. Oil stocks usually suffer from recession as the wheels of the economy come to a halt and there is less need to run industrial equipment and transportation. It is common for these stocks to fall more than the market indexes, so each stock in these sectors requires stop loss orders.

How Stop Loss Orders Would Have Saved Your Investment in 2008

In early 2008, many of the large banks and brokerage firm stocks began to fall by more than normal. Of course, no one could have predicted how bad the economy was going to get and how terribly many companies would eventually do. A year later, in 2009, some of these companies traded below 5 dollars a share and a few disappeared! But if you had used carefully placed stop loss orders in 2008, you might have saved yourself from incurring as much as 60% or 70% of the decline that followed.

At What Price to Set Your Stop Loss Orders

How much decline should you withstand?

It is crucial for investors to place stop loss orders at the right price level. This is where most investors make mistakes. Investors commonly set stop loss orders too close to the current trading price. In these cases, the stock declines a "normal" amount and the stock is sold, but it then recovers and advances to a new high. The investor has thus missed out on the gain. He or she has sold at the low, lost money, and missed the opportunity! This can be a frustrating experience and gives the use of stop loss orders a very bad name.

The real intent in using stop loss orders is not to mitigate short-term, temporary fluctuations due to normal market volatility, but to avoid catastrophic declines in a stock, sector or in the whole market. These generally occur during economic recessions that lead us into a bear market. This a time when investors punish the most economically sensitive stocks the most. This means that the price point at which you set your stop loss orders must be based on knowledge of the normal volatility of the stock or sector so you do not mistake a short-term blip for a serious long-term decline.

Every company and sector has its own unique pattern of volatility. If you look at the one-year chart of any stock or sector, you can see a visible pattern of ups and downs. The declining periods are usually associated with normal corrections in the overall market. These corrections are not of concern to you as they are usually only 8–10% drops. In most healthy bull markets, indexes experience these types of corrections 3 or 4 times a year. They usually last 4 to 6 weeks and are followed by the market going to even higher new highs. The "dips" are, in fact, opportunities for those underinvested to increase their stock exposure.

The key to effectively using stop loss orders is therefore to put them below where a normal correction might take the stock or sector. For example, if Company ABC stock typically declines 9% in a normal market correction, you want to make sure that your stop loss order is below that level so you can avoid the frustration of being stopped out too early and at the wrong price. But if each stock has its own patterns and volatility, how can you know where the stop loss order should be set? The next section explains how I approach this.

Using Charts, Beta, and Science to Figure Out the Stop Loss Price

Taking the guesswork out of stop loss orders

I treat the use of stop loss orders as a science. Through the use of technical analysis tools, I begin by studying the chart of each investment. This work helps identify how "normal" market volatility has historically affected each stock. That allows me to make an intelligent future assumption about how far the stock may decline in a normal market correction.

In addition, I use a formula that includes a mathematical concept called beta, which is a relative measure of volatility. This metric can be found very easily. Every publicly traded stock has a calculated beta, which acts as a relative measure because it tells us how volatile one stock is in comparison to the overall market. The market beta is always 1. A stock with a beta of 1.2 is 20% more volatile than the market, while a stock with

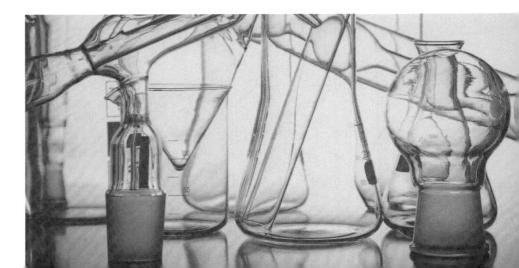

a beta of .8 is 20% less volatile than the market. This understanding and utilization of beta is another important tool in setting our stop losses correctly.

In the end, I set stop loss orders taking into account those two elements. First, stocks with a beta of 1 will experience the same level of volatility as the market in general, so I place stop loss orders slightly below their normal variance. In this way, I am already accounting for an 8 to 10% drop and will not sell the stock unless it goes below that normal volatility.

Meanwhile, by understanding that individual stocks with a higher volatility than the market will likely decline more than the market, I know I should keep my stop loss orders well below the normal correction level. Stocks with higher than normal beta "jump around" a lot further than your average stock, and this needs to be addressed when placing stop loss orders.

Tech stocks have traditionally been in the camp of being more volatile than normal. I usually have those stop loss orders further away from the current price for that reason. I want these types of companies to have a lot of room for volatility swings and avoid being stopped out too soon. On the other hand, industrial companies typically have patterns of volatility and beta lower than the market, meaning they are more stable in their valuations. As such, our stop loss price is usually closer to their current trading price because any fluctuation downwards could mean trouble.

Managing Your Stop Loss Orders

They need constant vigilance for resetting the price point

Stop loss orders need careful monitoring and management because the market is dynamic and always changing. News may affect the company or maybe its earnings will be reported soon. Once the stop loss order is set, it may need adjusting as the market and the stock move up or down.

If the market rises and your stocks advance, you need to recalibrate your stop loss orders accordingly to maintain the risk of catastrophic loss, but now at a higher level. This is called trailing stop loss orders. You want the stop loss to protect your newfound profits so you need to move the stop loss price upward.

Some investors do this automatically, programming their stop loss orders to increase by the same percentage amount as each gain. But I suggest doing this manually because I prefer to use each opportunity to change the stop as a time to review my original analysis of the company's beta and technical patterns and analysis. Sometimes this work will lead to a decision to change the percentage distance from the current price of the stop loss orders. For example, in the early days of Google's existence, the stock was highly volatile and a stop loss order needed to be very far away to avoid selling the stock during normal volatility. But as the company matured, the stock became less volatile, enabling me to put the stop loss order closer to its current trading price.

The Achilles Heel of Stop Loss Orders

You can't catch a speeding bullet

Tthere is a small risk in using stop loss orders in a rapidly declining market. The stop order may not stop things fast enough. When markets, sectors or stocks decline by more than normal, trades are often occurring rapidly. Your stop loss may have been initiated automatically when the low price you set was reached, but the brokerage company has to send in the "market order" to sell the shares. Once this order is received the stock is sold, but the market may have already declined further, and your sale will occur at an even lower price.

During normal market conditions and in the case of very liquid (high volume) stocks, the selling price may at least be quite close to the price indicated in the original stop loss instructions. However, during times of extreme volatility—whether it is for a single stock, a sector or the whole market—stocks can decline very rapidly and the number of investors lined up to sell can get long. In these cases, your stop loss order may be executed much lower than the original stop price.

But even then, you can probably be thankful, as large and extreme volume declines are typically the beginning of something worse, such as a bear market, a sector in trouble (like oil), or an individual company announcing very bad news. In most of these cases the market, sector or individual stock eventually falls much lower than the price at which you ended up selling your stock—and you will be glad that you had the stop loss order.

On the other hand, there are instances when well-conceived stop losses get executed below their set prices on heavy market volume and declining price, but then the stock bounces back immediately. This can happen during an abnormal and extreme temporary market decline, followed by an immediate recovery. These instances are rare, but they do happen, such as in May of 2010 when the overall market plunged 1000 points (about 7%) but recovered fully within minutes. In recent years, stock exchange officials are working on ways to curb these anomalies to protect investors.

There are several ways to mitigate the risk of this short-term extreme volatility:

- Don't use stop loss orders on all sectors.

- Depending on market cycle, consider using stop loss orders on half or just a third of the shares you own.

- Make sure to invest in very liquid stocks that are traded at a high volume of shares each day to ensure that there is always someone who wants to buy your shares.

- Continually monitor the stock prices and the stop loss levels—and adjust accordingly.

Case Studies of Active Risk Management

How stop loss orders would have helped investors

Here are a variety of examples of the value of using active asset allocation, sector management, and stop loss orders to minimize potentially huge losses during disastrous market crashes.

Overall Market Crash in 2008

As you probably recall, in the crash of 2008 the market lost nearly 50% of its value. If you had been using a combination of active asset allocation, sector management, and stop loss orders, you would have been able to preserve your portfolio from enormous losses as you probably would have recognized the need to sell your holdings in early 2008, after which most stocks and market indexes declined 45–60%.

Sector Catastrophes

There have been major sector crashes as well in recent history. An active risk management program would have preserved your portfolio in each of the following cases:

- If you had sold your bank and brokerage stocks in early 2008, you would have avoided a decline of 50–70%.

- If you owned material stocks in 2013, an active risk management process would have avoided the decline of 30% that occurred towards the end of the year.

- If you owned oil stocks in 2014, active risk management would have prevented you from losing up to 50% in their decline.

Overall Market Crash in 2008

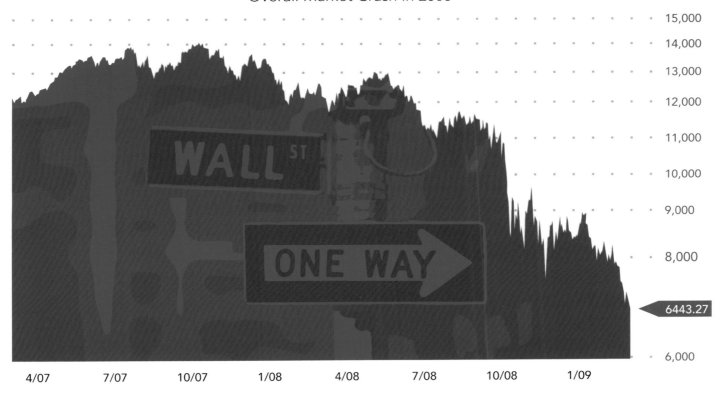

6443.27

| 4/07 | 7/07 | 10/07 | 1/08 | 4/08 | 7/08 | 10/08 | 1/09 |

Well-placed stop loss orders might have saved many investors losses of up to 50% of their portfolio wealth in the 2008 stock market collapse that took the Dow Jones average from its high of 14,164.43 in October 2007 to its low of 6443 in March 2009.

Individual stocks

There have been many major individual company crashes as well in recent history. An active risk management program would have preserved your portfolio in each of these cases.

Here are a few:

IBM: 2013

-60% from high

NOKIA: 2007

-90% from high

FREEPORT McMORAN: 2013

-90% from high

WASHINGTON MUTUAL: 2008

Out of business—100% loss

LEHMAN BROTHERS: 2008

Out of business—100% loss

VOLKSWAGEN: 2015

-50% from high

A Caveat about Robo-Investing (Part 2)

No risk management

We discussed robo-investing on page 157 and let's revisit its problems. It's hard to believe that investors would invest aggressively in the stock market without a "plan B" should it all come to a crashing halt. Investors must recall that we can have stock market declines of 35 –55%. It takes time for stocks to recoup large losses—on average, six to seven years.

Despite the increasing popularity of passive / robo- / index investing, I suggest taking heed of this warning. You need to employ risk management tools and a plan for avoiding catastrophic loss. I suggest you continue to invest with an eye towards growth, yet be well prepared with sound risk management tools such as stop loss orders should things go awry.

There Is Nothing Funny about Building Wealth

A nickel ain't worth a dime anymore. —YOGI BERRA

Everyone wants to ride with you in the limo, but what you want is someone who will take the bus with you when the limo breaks down. —OPRAH WINFREY

If inflation continues to soar, you're going to have to work like a dog just to live like one. —GEORGE GOBEL

Too many people spend money they earned . . . to buy things they don't want . . . to impress people that they don't like. —WILL ROGERS

I just bought a small condo overlooking the water. The water is in a cup, one floor below my unit. —JAROD KINTZ

Money doesn't buy you happiness, but you need to attain the money to realize that. —BARRY GORDI

The safe way to double your money is to fold it over once and put it in your pocket. —FRANK HUBBARD

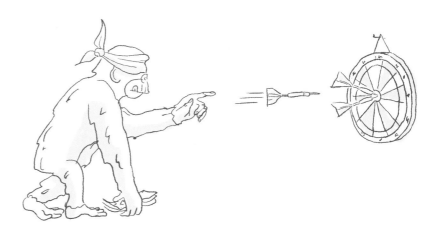

Bull markets are so fantastic that a monkey with a dart board and a list of stocks can make money. —ANONYMOUS

CHAPTER NINE

Non-Stock Market Investments

THE BOND MARKET, MY GRANDMOTHER AND THE FOUR HORSEMEN

> " We don't have to be smarter than the rest. We have to be more disciplined that the rest.
>
> —*Warren Buffett* "

Throughout this book, I have focused on investing in the stock market because it offers the highest potential returns for investors seeking to build wealth. But if you recall, I said earlier that you need to match your investment goals with the rate of return (ROR) that you can tolerate. For most investors, this means that you do not want to put all your money into the stock market, but rather invest some of it in other instruments, especially bonds.

This chapter will explore the world of bonds and bond alternatives, teaching you the basics to understand how they function, and what factors determine whether you might invest a portion of your money in bonds.

The Seemingly Safe World of Bonds

They are not just for "old" people

Bonds are the most traditional and common alternative investment to the stock market. High quality bonds—often called fixed income—carry less risk than stocks and provide a stream of income over a set period of time.

Such bond investments are structured similar to a loan in which the investor lends money to a corporation, municipality or government with an agreed-upon interest rate over a specific time period. Upon the maturity of that time period, the lendee (the institution borrowing the money) repays the investor their original capital plus the interest.

Historically, the rates of return on high quality bonds are in between stock market returns and money market funds. Bonds have less risk than stocks and therefore provide lower returns. However, they pose more risk than money market funds so they offer higher than money market yields. The main risk to bondholders lies in the ability for the lendee to be able to pay the interest payment on time and in full, and, most importantly, return all of the original principal at maturity date. Yes, there are lendees that fail, go out of business, or go bankrupt, but these tend to be far and few between.

How can you know if a bond offering is too risky? There are several high profile rating agencies that rate bonds. These agencies evaluate each bond based on the lendee's perceived ability to meet the terms of the agreement. A bond which has the highest likelihood of meeting the terms is deemed AAA while those with lesser quality are rated AA, A . . . BBB, BB, B and the lettering continues downward. At the bottom of the ladder are bonds whose stability has reached the lowest point, often referred to as "junk" bonds. These are so risky that, from time to time, investors lose all of their principal.

So the credit quality of bonds is very important for those investors who want to stay conservative. Of course, as in all things, there is no free lunch. Those bonds with the most stellar credit quality pay the least interest and those with the worst credit risk pay the most! You get paid to assume risk in the bond market—just as you do in the stock market or anything else in life!

How Bonds Are Sold

Face value vs. par value

Bonds are often sold according to a "face value," an amount that the bond will be worth when it matures. The price an investor pays for a bond is its par value or the current market value of the bond.

For example, a company might offer a one-year 2% $1000 bond for $950 with a 7.3% yield to maturity. The investor will receive 2% in interest over the year and then get $1,000 at maturity. The extra 5.3% is the $50 difference between par and face value.

Why Bond Prices Fluctuate

Bond prices move inversely to Interest rates

As you know, interest rates fluctuate on a daily basis. This introduces a level of "interest rate risk" when it comes to investing in bonds. When interest rates move in one direction or the other, it has a tendency to cause the price of bonds to move in the opposite direction to compensate for the change.

- Rising interest rates have a long history of pushing bond prices downward. This occurs because investors often sell bonds when interest rates rise in anticipation of buying different higher yielding bonds either now or in the future.

- Declining interest rates, on the other hand, have the exact opposite effect—pushing the price of bonds upward because more investors now want higher-paying bonds.

These gyrations in pricing are minimal for short maturity bonds, i.e., those coming due within 5 years. But the pricing differentials can be dramatic for long-term maturity bonds, i.e., those beyond 15 years. It is possible that a long-term bondholder could sustain a temporary decline of 15–30 percent when the interest rates are rising, even though the bond itself may have high credit quality!

Of course at maturity, investors holding that bond will be returned their original principle plus the interest. However, in the intermediate period of time, which can be many years, they will experience a reduction in the value of their bonds and the sinking feeling that comes with it. Also, if the interest rates have risen, an investor may have also lost the opportunity to invest in a higher paying bond.

Our view is that if an investor can handle this level of volatility, they are better served by owning stocks as opposed to long-term bonds. Therefore, unless you know for sure or feel that the odds are very high that interest rates will stay low or go lower the most conservative bond investors stick with high-quality bonds with short to intermediate maturities of 1–15 years at most.

Taxes on Bonds Impact Your Return

You can't escape the IRS with most bonds

In analyzing the bond market, one must consider not only the rate of a bond's payout at various maturities, and where interest rates are headed, but also the tax implications for you. This last element is as important as the first two, because your tax rate can greatly impact the return on a bond. Unless your investment assets are in a non-taxable account such as an IRA, it is important to calculate the actual after-tax yield in order to compare bonds and determine which one(s) are best for you.

Most municipal bonds are not taxed at the federal or state level, which makes them a good bargain. However, these bonds often pay very low interest rates, so even with no taxes, the return is minimal.

US Treasury bonds are free from federal tax though not state taxes. This often makes them a good investment, especially if someone lives in a state with a low or no state income tax.

Corporate bonds are taxed at both the federal and state level. However, corporate bonds usually pay the highest interest rates, so even after taxes, the returns can be high.

The Four Horsemen

Alternatives to bonds for non-stock portion of portfolios

There are times when bonds are not the best investment for the non-stock portion of a portfolio. Let's use the period of 2008 to 2016 as a case study, but the analysis here pertains to any period of time with similar conditions.

From 2008 to 2016, interest rates were at historically low levels due to the global recession. In response to the financial and economic meltdown, the Federal Reserve and other global central banks dramatically lowered interest rates

in an effort to revive economic growth. This strategy worked and the economy eventually recovered, though at a much slower pace than prior economic recoveries and expansions. However, given the tepid recovery, many global central banks were unwilling to raise their interest rates for fear that it would reduce or stop the recovery. As a result, over nearly a decade, we witnessed one of the longest periods of very low interest rates in our lifetime. Though this situation was great for borrowers—think low mortgage rates—it had the opposite effect for bond buyers because low interest rates drive up bond prices, which reduces their eventual returns.

Consider, for example, that a 5-year Treasury bond had a current annual yield of just 1.6%. This return was abnormally low and would accomplish little to help most investors achieve their long-term financial planning goals. In contrast, the historical yield for a 5-year Treasury bond has been more in the range of 4 to 6%, a return that at least provides a decent value as an alternative to far riskier stock market exposure.

In short, the bond market in times like 2008 to 2016 provided little value for sophisticated investors seeking higher returns along with some degree of safety for a portion of their portfolio. Not only were the returns of little value, but there was also a significant interest rate risk given that interest rates at some point would rise, driving down bond prices, which would create losses for current bond holders. For investors who own bond mutual funds, these can be an especially dangerous period of time. Unlike individual bonds, bond funds have no maturity dates. Therefore, bond funds on the whole will decline throughout a rising interest rate environment and will not return to their previous levels until rates fall back to their original starting levels. This could take decades or more given how low rates are today.

Given the above points, bonds are not always a viable alternative for the "bulk" of the non-stock portion of an investor's portfolio. So what is an investor to do as an alternative to the bond market when bond returns are ultra-low? Where can investors go to find investments that could yield better results than the bond market without subjecting some portion of their portfolios to the volatility and risk correlations of the stock market?

I thank my grandmother for teaching me the best answers to this conundrum. She was a smart lady who didn't like the volatility of the stock market and considered it too risky and unpredictable, so she invested wisely elsewhere. Her goal was to generate income and return without the volatility of the stock market. Some of her portfolio was invested in bonds, but she also invested in four other investment classes that have little correlation to the stock market, making them less volatile.

Preferred Stocks

These are a type of stock that differs from the "common" stock that most investors buy and sell. Preferred stocks are a sort of hybrid stock in between regular stocks (equities) and debt instruments (bonds). They rank higher in their rights to a company's assets than common stock, but lower than bonds. In the event the company pays out dividends, all preferred stock owners must be paid first before common stock owners receive dividends. If the company goes bankrupt, bond holders get paid on their investment first, then preferred stock owners are compensated for their equity investment, and last to be paid are common stock owners if there is any money left over.

As such, preferred stocks have less risk than common stocks, but not quite as much stability as bonds. Preferred stocks are traded over the stock exchanges, just as common stocks are. As with bonds, there are agencies that rate preferred stocks, so investors can assess whether a preferred stock is safe or not. In short, preferred stocks can be a safer way to invest in companies to earn higher returns than bonds, but with less risk than common stocks. High quality preferred stocks often pay 4–6% dividends.

Utility Stocks

Utilities are those companies that provide communities with their water, electrical power, gas, and other basic needs. Owning stock in these companies is not very different than owning stock in any other company, except for one thing: utility companies tend to pay high dividends year after year. While these stocks don't appreciate much in value, their dividend payout can amount to what investors receive from the best paying bonds when the bond market is healthy, on the level of 3% to 7%.

Why do utility companies pay such high dividends? The main reason is that they serve the general public with key services that must be provided at all times. In general, local, regional, or state governments do not want to encourage competition for utilities as this would lead to chaos with water and gas pipes, as well as electric lines. As a result, utility companies are somewhat protected against competition, and this reduces their expenses, allowing them to have higher earnings with which to pay dividends.

Real Estate Investment Trust (REIT)

A REIT is a company that invests in income-producing real estate, such as shopping malls, office parks, hospitals, apartment complexes, student dormitories, and more. The REIT then pays out its income in the form of dividends to shareholders who have invested in the company, just like common stock owners. REITs may either invest directly in income-producing properties or in mortgages. The advantage of a REIT is that it usually pays high dividends, and when the real estate market is doing well, there is less risk than with stocks, making them a good conservative investment for the alternative portion of a portfolio.

Master Limited Partnerships (MLPs)

These are partnerships that invest in businesses, and investors can buy stock and become one of the limited partners. The MLPs pay out the majority of their earnings in the form of dividends to the limited partners. Most MLPs are focused on energy businesses, such as pipelines, oil or gas exploration and production, and fuel storage facilities, but there are other industries as well such as amusement parks, cemeteries, and others. MLPs are traded on the stock markets, making it easy to buy into them. MLPs also pay dividends between 4% and 6%.

• • •

Over the past few years, these asset classes have worked exceedingly well as a bond alternative. What's more, during the same period, there was also a significant increase in the principal value of some of these investments. This is unusual for these traditionally conservative, yield-oriented investments since they are not growth companies that have accelerating earnings. The rise of principle in some of these assets classes beyond just their bond-like interest and dividends payments was a welcome surprise.

PRINCIPLE 17

RIDE THE FOUR HORSEMEN OF ALTERNATIVE
ASSET ALLOCATION WHEN NECESSARY

These four key asset classes, which I often refer to as the "four horsemen," have become a key component of my alternate allocations since 2008, largely to replace what I often would have invested in bonds. These asset classes have little correlation to the stock market, meaning they have much less risk while providing yields ranging from 3% to 7%. When I invest in them, I am not expecting to see exceptional appreciation of their stock values, but they are perfect for the more conservative portion of an investor's portfolio. They help provide stability through their generally predictable dividend and interest payments.

Research Is the Key to Finding Alternatives to Bonds

As it is with everything in investing

As I have reinforced throughout this book, the key to investing is research. Each of these horseman carry inherent business risk that must be studied carefully. One cannot take anything for granted, even for instruments that are often thought of as very safe conservative investments, such as utilities, REITs, or MLPs.

For example, consider electric utility companies. They are often viewed as very predictable businesses when it comes to earning profits and paying out consistently high dividends. Each month, they pump out electricity, then send consumers a bill to pay. However, it takes a large investment in infrastructure to deliver electricity to homes and businesses. There can be complications or disasters. In 2010, electrical fires took lives and destroyed homes in San Bruno, California. That sent Pacific Gas & Electric (PG&E) stock tumbling.

It is therefore important to study every investment, no matter how safe it may appear or how good a historical record it has. Even conservative, predictable investments can have hidden risks.

Diversifying Your Alternative Bond Investments

Don't ride just one horse

The importance of diversification cannot be underestimated. If you invest in any of the four horsemen as part of your alternative investments, be sure to select several companies from each one so you can mitigate the risk. Do not dump a lump sum into one preferred stock, or one utility, or one REIT or MLP. Always research and choose several different companies for each asset class of the four horsemen.

Finally, when building a portfolio of investments that provide dividends and /or interest, don't let greed drive your decisions, becoming what I call a "yield chaser." On average, any of the high quality horseman yields 3–6%. If you find a REIT with a 15% yield, don't automatically buy it in a knee jerk reaction, trusting that its returns will continue at that rate. Stop and conduct thorough research as to why the REIT did so well in a given year

before going further. If it looks too good to be true, it probably is.

As I hope you have learned throughout this book, I believe strongly that there is no "free lunch" in the investment business. Extraordinarily high yields come with extraordinarily high risk. Usually a high yield is a sign that a business is in trouble. Often high yield investments are very volatile and as a result, sometimes cease paying any interest or dividends at all because they collapse from having had too high a payout in the past.

Though the four horseman have worked like a charm over the last few years, and have been far less risky and volatile than stocks, they are not bonds and still carry some risks as described here. The biggest risk is unknown events in the future that might negatively impact these companies. Therefore, out of prudence, I use a stop loss order on these bond alternatives, just as I do for equity investments. For example, using stop loss orders came in very handy in 2014 when I sold MLPs due to the crash in the energy market.

For the most part, it is clear that investors have done very well with these four asset classes over bonds. Why? Typically, these asset classes show little fluctuation over most economic cycles. However, every economic cycle is very different and so going into the future, nothing can be guaranteed.

I am always reminded of the old adage . . . you can buy what you think is a great investment, but you have to keep looking at the future because nothing will increase in value unless other investors buy it after you! Growth stocks usually trade upward for a simple reason. Their continued earnings growth attracts more and more investors and the rising demand for shares lifts the price. But what about our horsemen—utility stocks, preferred stocks, MLPs and REITs? They have slow growth, not accelerating earnings growth, which is why they rarely rise in value.

But what investors experienced from 2008–2016 was a level of demand for yield that has never been seen before. During that period, more and more investors came to this conclusion about the four horseman and invested billions in these same companies, pushing their values upward. This demand for yield is the sole reason we witnessed a rise in their value. Anyone who recognized early on that interest rates would stay low and that these typically boring conservative horseman would provide a fantastic alternative to the bond market was definitely lucky. When it comes to investing, it's good to be involved in the early stages of a long-term trend.

Returning to Bonds

They will come back, for sure!

Bond alternatives work well in periods of low and declining interest rates for the reasons laid out in this chapter. However, when interest rates rise, sometimes these investments can come under selling pressure, causing their values to decline. This selling pressure is usually a result of the wise investors who realize that rising interest rates eventually make the bond market attractive again.

For example, if a 5-year Treasury bond, which currently yields around 1% annually, rises to 4% due to a general rise in all rates, this starts to look more appealing than the four horseman—which inherently have higher risk.

During periods when the interest rate rises—as is happening today—it is the right time for investors to reduce their use of the four horsemen alternatives and return to buying bonds. This change would help them avoid the potential significant decline in the value of these bond alternatives due to higher interest rates, and instead provide them with the tried-and-true conservative position that bonds offer with their traditional 3–6% yields.

CHAPTER TEN

How *to* Keep *the* Wealth Management Process Going

7 KEYS TO MAINTAINING GROWTH TO ACHIEVE YOUR ROR

> " It's not how much money you make, but how much money you keep, how hard it works for you, and how many generations you keep it for.
>
> —*Robert Kiyosaki* "

You've come a long way since opening this book to learn about creating wealth and investing. So far, you've learned about the need to invest in the stock market to achieve the type of returns that most investors need to build wealth. I examined the history of the stock market to understand its volatility, but at the same time, history confirms that, of all investment instruments, stocks produce the greatest returns over the long term. I next looked at how you estimate your wealth needs for the future and, as a result, how to calculate the rate of return (ROR) you need to achieve your goals either to have enough money to last throughout your lifetime and future generations, or, if you are an institutional investor, to create a portfolio that will meet your organization's spending policy.

I then shared the concept of a **SMART** asset allocation plan, avoiding mutual funds, index funds, ETFs, and other investment instruments that either charge fees that deplete your earnings or seldom meet expectations. I also reviewed why modern portfolio theory is outdated in today's chaotic world, where the "set it and forget it" philosophy no longer works. Instead, I discussed how today's **SMART** investors must seek to maximize earnings and avoid the downturns, through an aggressive, pro-active management of their portfolio, buying and selling stocks in accordance with market conditions in the context of their ROR.

I next examined how you can learn to understand and read business market cycles so that you can select stocks based on an informed sense of where the stock market is very likely to be going. In this context, you can invest to stay ahead of the market curve rather than trailing it. I also examined how economic recessions affect the stock market and the ugly math of bear markets. Understanding the stock market cycle can be invaluable in knowing when to re-enter the market ahead of other investors in order to capture the maximum amount of profit as the market rises.

I discussed sector investing, another key strategy for the **SMART** investor. By learning to invest in the right sectors as they rise and fall according to economic cycles, you can maximize each of your stock selections for the greatest profit potential, as well as know when to sell stocks that are about to tumble in a coming economic cycle downturn. I cannot emphasize enough how understanding bull and bear markets, and taking appropriate and timely actions to improve your stock portfolio, can substantially increase your wealth and mitigate your risk.

I next taught you the seven fundamental analysis indicators—the advanced tools for **SMART** investing. Using these ratios and calculations—Debt, Debt/Equity ratio, Price/Earnings ratio (P/E), Return on Equity (ROE),

Earnings Growth Rate, Price/Earnings to Growth rate (PEG), and Price/Sales ratio—you can substantially improve your research in companies that are worth investing in, versus those you want to avoid.

We reviewed ways to protect your investment using stop loss orders as a third element of my active risk management program. And I reviewed what to do with the portion of your money that you do not put into stocks, but rather into alternative investments, including bonds and any of the four horsemen (preferred stocks, utilities, REITs, and master limited partnerships).

This chapter is the final key to your investor education—how to keep building your wealth over the long term. I will explore seven key concepts for continuously maximizing your investments and avoiding loss of profits and principal.

Happiness is not in the mere possession of money;
it lies in the joy of achievement, in the thrill of creative effort.
—FRANKLIN D. ROOSEVELT

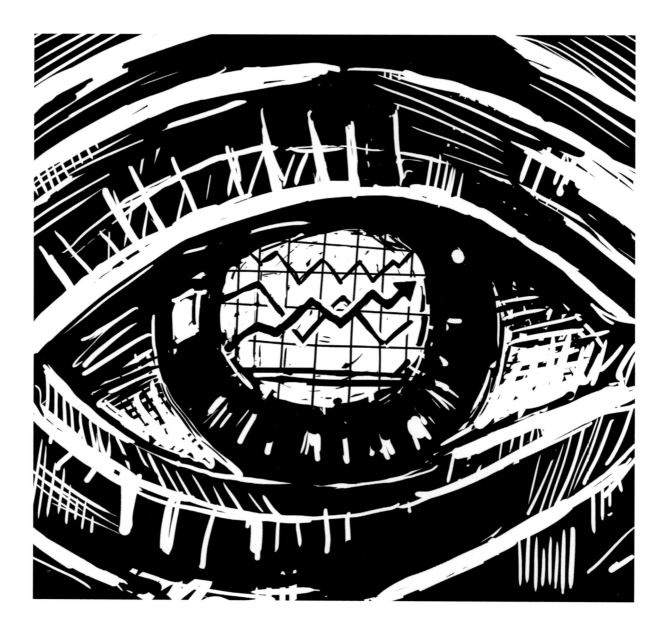

Here are the seven keys to maintaining a strategic and successful wealth building program:

1 Keep an Eye on the Business Cycle

SMART investors never let their guard down. It is vital to keep watching the economy to see where we are in the business cycle—whether the economy is in expansion or contraction. Keep in mind that business cycles last, on average, 7 to 9 years and follow a fairly predictable pattern.

Let's say that we are starting in a period of expansion at the current time. We can expect the expansion to move the economy upwards until a point at which it peaks. Then, for various reasons, the economy will invariably begin to weaken, and we enter a period of contraction, until at some point we hit a low point, called the trough. This might lead to a period of recession or a depression. However, the economy always seems to recover, and begin an upward swing to a new period of expansion. Research shows that in the past 50 years, periods of expansion tend to last far longer than periods of contraction.

Understanding the business cycle is invaluable because we know that the stock market goes through cycles that precede the business cycle. Recall the chart on page 120 which shows how stocks rise and fall just slightly ahead of

---

PRINCIPLE 18

YOU CAN'T STOP MONITORING YOUR INVESTMENTS

My philosophy is that you cannot take a "set it and forget it" approach to your portfolio. Global financial markets operate 24/7. You need to maintain a proactive stance, continually evaluating your investments, looking for opportunities to maximize profits and avoid downturns, and use the knowledge and tools I have shared in this book. Over time, there are always opportunities to buy new stocks that will perform better than other investments in your portfolio that are becoming stale. There are regular swings in the business cycle that impact different sectors and industries, and monitoring these will help you make SMART decisions about when to buy or sell investments.

the business cycle. **SMART** investors closely follow the business cycle and add to or reduce their stock exposure in expectation of where the business cycle is going. This knowledge allows them to buy stocks that will profit from a coming expansion and sell stocks that will lose value in a coming recession. In effect, watching the business cycle improves your investment timing so you can maximize profits and minimize losses. So be sure to look for clues about the business cycle.

One way to do such research is to read the leading daily business-oriented newspapers such as *The Wall Street Journal, New York Times* and *The Financial Times*. Weekly and monthly must-reads also include *Barron's* and *The Economist*.

Following research analysts and economic reports is also critical to staying up to speed. Look for statistics about the growth of GDP, unemployment rates, retail sales, car sales, and other indicators of an economic expansion or the start of a contraction. And, finally, keep in mind the following key principles about business cycles:

- When the economy is coming out of a recession, it is the perfect time to get into the stock market to profit from the coming growth.

- Don't let fear of a bear market override investing during the first years of an expansion.

- Historically, expansions have lasted longer than recessions; if you expect an expansion to occur, it will usually be a good long run for profit making.

As soon as you begin to see the signs of a contraction or coming recession, take action to sell those stocks that are most susceptible to the downturn.

② Keep Watching the Sectors

In addition to following the business cycle, **SMART** investors must continuously track the sectors in which they have invested and take note of how each sector's movement correlates with the economy. History shows that there are specific patterns among sectors to rise and fall according to the business cycle.

Review the chart on page 154 again and take note of these distinctive patterns. When the economy heats up, the entire asset class of stocks tends to rise, especially telecoms, technology, industrials, and consumer discretionary companies. As the business cycle matures, many of these sectors eventually become overvalued and the threat of recession begins to loom. It is at this point that companies with consistent growth not tied to the economy will shine and their stock prices perform well. Consumer staples, healthcare and utility stocks are good examples.

To maintain a solid strategy of wealth building, it is thus critical to pay attention to the sectors. Watch the news and follow the analysts every day for information about the asset classes and industry sectors in which you are invested. Follow the leading companies in your favorite

sectors as they may be harbingers of good or bad news for other companies in the same industry. As soon as you see news that portends potential problems among many companies in a certain industry, take steps to mitigate the risk that you could be invested in a bad sector.

③ Always Use Fundamental Analysis on Individual Companies

Paying attention to the business cycle and keeping an eye on the sectors is not usually enough to avert a disastrous loss or to miss out on a substantial profit making opportunity. You also need to keep monitoring the key fundamentals of each of your stocks. Has any company's performance changed since you bought its stock? Has its P/E gone up or down? What about its earnings growth rate or price-to-earnings growth (PEG) rate?

Above all, pay attention to company earnings for stocks you own. Keep an earnings calendar that shows which company will report earnings on what day and time. It is critical to pay attention to these earnings announcements and listen to the earnings conference calls. These reports let us know if the company is executing their business plan and keeping up with expectations, as well new strategic developments.

Keep in mind that the majority of investors are driven by emotions, especially greed and fear, and can often bid the price of a stock far too high, overvaluing it beyond its projected earnings or its growth potential, or far too low, undervaluing it given its potential earnings growth. By using the ratios and tools of fundamental analysis, however, you can gain deeper insights into the potential of your investments to rise or fall. This allows you to make more informed decisions about whether you should sit tight on a stock, or whether it may be time to buy more of it or even to start selling it.

Fundamental analysis especially helps you identify new companies to invest in that might have better prospects than your current portfolio

of stocks. As you watch the economic cycle and sectors, you may find companies whose return on equity (ROE) or earnings growth rate outperforms some of your current stock holdings. If so, it could be time to alter your portfolio, selling those investments that have hit their peak, and buying new stocks that have greater potential for appreciation.

4 Look out for new ideas and trends

The business world is an ever-changing, dynamic system, composed of companies

constantly seeking to fulfill the needs of consumers and other companies that will pay for their products and services. Companies are thus constantly inventing new things or improving existing products. Investors must keep following the news and analysts about the companies they invest in. I also recommend following the news on competitors. You never know when a new product will suddenly become the latest fad and sweep the market in some specific field. If you already own stock in that company, it could produce a huge profit windfall for you, but if you own stock in a competitor who cannot offer the same new product or innovation, it could lead to a major hit on their stock price.

Most importantly, be on the lookout for new companies that have recently gone public following an initial public offering (IPO). I do not believe it is usually a **SMART** investment strategy to chase IPO stocks in their first days. There is often a lot of hype behind an IPO that artificially inflates the price of these stocks, and the first months of an IPO can be an unstable period when the stock price fluctuates with market moods. I prefer to wait a month or even a full quarter to assess a new IPO company's fundamentals accurately and assess its earnings and growth potential.

5 **Be sure to regularly adjust your stop losses**

As discussed, stop loss orders should not remain stagnant in a dynamic market. This means that as the price of each stock in your portfolio rises, you must consistently and continuously reset the stop loss orders to a new point that correlates with the higher average stock price. I recommend that you review your stop loss orders each week to update those that need resetting. Be sure to set the orders far enough away from each stock's normal range of downward volatility. You don't want to prematurely sell a stock that is simply undergoing a bad day, if, ultimately, that stock is worth owning over the long term.

6 **Watch your spending in your own budget**

Pay attention to your expenditures relative to what you originally planned on spending when you calculated your ROR based on your long-term goals for yourself and your family. Once you begin building wealth, there is often a tendency to lose control of your budgeting. With more money and greater independence, many people believe they can "upgrade" the lifestyle they had been planning to live, and so they indulge themselves in pleasurable rewards, new purchases, upgrades, and improvements.

The problem is that if you are spending additional money and taking it from your principal, you will alter the rate of return you need to achieve your wealth goals. Let's assume you spend an additional $25,000, $50,000, or $100,000 beyond your normal spend rate for several years, taking the money from your investment account for which you required a 6% return to meet your wealth goals. These extra expenditures might easily boost your required ROR from 6% to 6.2% or 6.5%—and even a small percentage increase like this will affect your long-term game plan. To compensate for the lost principal, you may need to alter your asset allocation, forcing you to take on greater exposure to the risks of the stock market to try to earn a higher rate of return.

So if you find yourself spending more than you planned for when you calculated your ROR and did your asset allocation, take stock of how this will impact your investment decisions. You must either reduce your spending to realign your lifestyle with your ROR, or you recalculate your ROR and possibly reassess your asset allocation and take a greater risk.

7 **To be good at this, you have to be passionate**

As you can see, maintaining a strategically sound and successful wealth building program takes knowledge, time, and effort. You can have an extremely profitable portfolio of equity investments at any given moment, just to see it collapse when

a downward business cycle that you weren't ready for begins, or when several of your key securities suddenly tumble after poor earnings reports. Investing takes knowledge and the proper skills (such as knowing how to do fundamental analysis), but it also takes vigilance to ensure that you are maximizing your potential for profits while

minimizing your risks. If you like doing this, then you will be good at it!

Perhaps the reason why so many investors fail to do well is related to their level of interest and effort. You can never be a ranked tennis player without putting in your practice time and being consistent day to day. The same is true of the successful investor; you really have to enjoy it to put in the time required. Otherwise, it will feel like work, and you are not going to want to do it regularly.

Many people say they prefer to invest on their own, but their focus in doing it comprehensively and well comes and goes in waves. They go through periods of great diligence in their investment research and trading, followed by periods of complete neglect. This may not be the best approach, of course, as it risks missing important news that could affect one's investments. If this is your pattern, you might want to recommit to being a **SMART** investor, or realize that you may simply need help from professionals.

Epilogue

I AM PASSIONATE ABOUT SUCCESSFUL investing and continually working to improve my knowledge that can help people enhance their wealth and enjoy the benefits that come with it. After reading this book, I hope I have provided you with knowledge about my process and investment style, and that you find it helpful in your own investing. As I conclude, there are a number of parting comments that I think are important.

The financial markets have changed dramatically over the last few decades. The old rules of investing no longer work. What were once tried and true theories have failed. Today's successful investor needs to put more effort into their investment success, as opposed to the old "buy and hold" notions of modern portfolio theory.

Investment performance is about selecting the right investments at the right time. It is also about keeping your overall portfolio costs low and having a portfolio that is transparent and understandable. This flies in contrast to the big Wall Street firms that often create portfolios for their clients utilizing many fund "products" that each have various expensive layers of fees embedded in them. To that add the cost of paying the firm's management fee.

Investing with a personal wealth plan and knowing your personal ROR (rate of return) is one of the key elements to successful investing. It allows you to establish what level of return you will need over the long term, and how much risk you will need to get there.

This brings us to the concept of risk. There is little question that we are in an era of heightened risk. As a savvy investor, you should not be taking any more risk than you require. As discussed throughout this book, risk can be easily determined. I have also discussed in detail how investors have a gross underestimation of risk and the likelihood and effects of catastrophic declines. I do not want you to be one of those investors. Establish the risk you require and then manage it. I hope my discussion of risk and the Active Risk Management process I recommend will help you become a savvy investor.

The human brain is not well geared for investing. Individual investors tend to get caught up in their emotions about markets, sectors and companies. They often refuse to abandon their "darlings"—companies they fall in love with and want to own stock in. It is important to take the human brain out of the equation by following a process that removes emotion and is based on a history of success. Investors who use the emotional side of their brain tend to buy high and sell low. I do not want you to be that investor.

Clearly this new era of investing requires in-depth research, time and experience. Success today requires a disciplined process and tools that can help manage risk and return. Many of the themes, processes and tools I expressed in this book require continuous vigilance to keep them up to date on a daily basis.

I am passionate about my work and hope that my passion is rubbing off on you. I hope you have learned a great deal about history, investing, risk and maybe even about yourself while reading this book. Wishing you investment success in the future!

Postscript: *A Note about My Social Philosophy*

Caring for humanity is as important as making money

ONE MIGHT THINK THAT EVERYONE loves a boom cycle. After all, these are times when people accumulate wealth. However, in the past several decades, we have been witnessing an increasing incongruity in the economic consequences of booms. Statistics show that fewer and fewer members of society benefit from the upward movement of both our economic and stock cycles, particularly in the US. This has created income inequalities at a disproportionate level that many economists believe are very unhealthy for a functional society.

It is clear to me that a financial system that improves the wealth of only a small percentage of a nation's population leads to serious economic, social, and political problems. History proves that a large and comfortable middle class is necessary to fuel a sustainably upward mobile society. When the majority of people in a nation have enough money to pay for their basic needs (housing, transportation, energy, food, and healthcare expenses) plus excess cash to buy consumer products and services, to travel, and even to invest, the overall economy improves and goes into a virtuous cycle of growth. But when the majority of people do not increase their wealth through employment, investing, and savings, it leads to a stagnant economy. This often leads a downward cycle of lower consumer spending, a drop in the production of goods and services, higher unemployment, and eventually the risk of a recession.

In a free market economy, there are many factors that contribute to the spread of wealth. These include:

- Providing cost-effective higher education and job training leading to higher-paying professional jobs for more people;

- Teaching people how to invest in **SMART** ways to make money in the financial markets;

- Facilitating entrepreneurialism and business startups as these foster innovation, new businesses, and jobs;

- Making reasonable interest rate loans available to the majority of people so they can use them to purchase homes, and reasonable rate credit cards so people can purchase goods and services and pay for them over time.

Similarly, there are many factors that detract from the spread of prosperity and lead to the unequitable distribution of assets—a "wealth gap."

These include:

- Unemployment, underemployment, or low wages that stifle consumer spending;

- A low savings and investment rate among the general population;

- Interest rates that are too low for the current economic conditions, because they tend to inspire a sharp rise in asset prices that put investment out of the reach of the population.

My view is that the business cycle and the market cycle must be tightly linked. When the Federal Reserve tries to boost the economy by lowering interest rates too far, those closest to the money flow (bankers, asset managers and wealthy investors) are the ones who benefit the most. On the other hand, when the Federal Reserve tries to slow the economy by raising interest rates too far, they can put the brakes on growth for everyone. There is, however, a balanced middle ground that must be found for each economic quarter.

There are serious repercussions in society when the wealth gap becomes too pronounced and unfair. Historically, vast inequalities of wealth were corrected violently, by revolutions like the French Revolution of 1789 or the Russian Revolution of 1917. Among developed Western nations today, closing the wealth gap is generally fought as a political battle over taxation as a form of wealth redistribution, and over government regulation of the financial industry.

In 2008, greed played a major role in causing the collapse of the banking system and thousands of US citizens took to the streets in unprecedented numbers to protest against the growing power and perks of the wealthy. The Occupy Wall Street movement in the US and the many labor strikes and protests in European nations were messages of a rising social unrest that we should not ignore.

As I said at the beginning of this book, I believe that a prosperous society benefiting everyone creates far better conditions to build sustainable growth and increase wealth for all citizens.

I owe a great many thanks to a number of people who helped
and supported me during the writing of this book:

First and foremost I thank my family—
Velda, Hudson and Stella
for supporting me through this process.

I thank my team at Main Street Research—
Tamra Stern JD CFP, Elizabeth Baldassari, Aaron Stern, Adrienne Coenen,
Charito Mittelman JD, Benjamin Armellini, Stephanie Hawk and Natalie McMahon.

I also must thank my clients, mentors and peers, who have provided me over the past several decades
with tremendous experiences, opportunities for knowledge, and fueling my passion for investing.

Finally, I thank my publisher Over And Above Creative—
Rick Benzel and Susan Shankin, for their editorial and design expertise,
and Tim Kummerow for his delightful artwork.
Together they have helped me bring this book to life for you to enjoy and learn from.

About the Author

JAMES E. DEMMERT has been managing investment portfolios for institutional and individual investors for over 30 years. He has experience in all aspects of investment management including equity and fixed income research, trading and portfolio management. He has particular expertise in macro-economic research and risk management and is responsible for his firm's Active Risk Management processes. He is a seasoned wealth manager and is experienced in the areas of retirement, financial, estate and tax planning.

Mr. Demmert has been a featured speaker for a number of public organizations, including the American Association of Individual Investors (AAII). He has authored numerous articles on finance and investment management and his work has appeared in many financial publications including *The Wall Street Journal*, *Barron's*, *BusinessWeek* and *Fortune*.

James' past experience includes positions with LF Rothschild and Lehman Brothers before founding Main Street Research, a registered investment advisor, in 1993. He graduated from Harvard University.

If we command our wealth, we shall be rich and free.
If our wealth commands us, we are poor indeed.
—EDMUND BURKE